KU-642-120

The harassment and abuse of older people in the private rented sector

Nancy Carlton, Frances Heywood, Misa Izuhara, Jenny Pannell, Tina Fear and Robin Means

The POLICY PRESS

First published in Great Britain in January 2003 by
The Policy Press
34 Tyndall's Park Road
Bristol BS8 1PY
UK

Tel +44 (0)117 954 6800
Fax +44 (0)117 973 7308
e-mail tpp@bristol.ac.uk
www.policypress.org.uk

British Library Cataloguing in Publication Data

A catalogue record for this book is available from the British Library

ISBN 1 86134 458 9 paperback

Nancy Carlton is Senior Lecturer in the Faculty of the Built Environment, University of the West of England, Bristol, **Frances Heywood** and **Misa Izuhara** are Research Fellows at the School for Policy Studies, University of Bristol, **Jenny Pannell** is Visiting Senior Research Fellow, **Tina Fear** is Senior Lecturer and **Robin Means** is Associate Dean (Research and International Development), all in the Faculty of Health and Social Care, University of the West of England, Bristol.

Cover design by Qube Design Associates, Bristol.
Printed and bound in Great Britain by Hobbs the Printers, Southampton

Contents

Acknowledgements

The authors would like to start by thanking all those older people who participated in this research. They would also like to thank all the informants and the extremely helpful Advisory Group to the project. The research would not have been possible without funding from Help the Aged. Finally, the quality of the research was greatly aided by the insightful comments and contributions of Jean Kysow, who acted as a specialist consultant to the research team.

Advisory Committee

Professor Anthea Tinker (Chair)
Professor of Social Gerontology
Age Concern Institute of Gerontology
King's College London

Nick Beacock
Manager of the Campaign for Bedsit Rights
Shelter

Paul Taylor
Manager of Shelterline
Shelterline

Dr Derek Hawes
Visiting Lecturer in Housing Practice and Policy
School for Policy Studies
University of Bristol

Professor Philip Leather
Professor of Housing
Centre for Urban and Regional Studies
University of Birmingham

Joe Oldman
Homelessness Strategy Coordinator
Help the Aged

Daniel Pearson
Special Projects Manager
Help the Aged

Kim Willcock
Research Officer
Help the Aged

Introduction

Rationale behind the research

This research arose from a concern that older people living in private rented housing were vulnerable to abuse and harassment by landlords. Help the Aged had funded voluntary agencies working with older people, and some agencies reported incidences of violence and other forms of harassment in private rented housing. There was concern that agencies offering advice, housing, health and social welfare were not reaching older private tenants.

However, the evidence was anecdotal, and there was no research which specifically focused on older private tenants. Existing research on the private rented sector has, indeed, been 'age-blind'. Much research on older people, particularly that on abuse and harassment, gave little consideration to where people were living, and no information on housing tenure.

Aims and objectives of this report

Prevalence studies are notoriously difficult in a field such as abuse or harassment, and raise sensitive ethical issues. Since it would not be possible to estimate the extent of landlord abuse and harassment, a qualitative research method was chosen to explore the experiences of older people in the private sector, and their relationships with private landlords, and statutory and voluntary agencies working in this field. The aims of the research include an analysis of the complex reasons why older people are living in private rented housing, whether by choice or as tenure of last resort. The great diversity of the private rented sector, and variations in market factors (such as property price differentials and supply and demand of housing) are also important issues to be examined. This report does not set out to imply that all older people are more vulnerable than anyone else to abusive behaviours, and recognises that most older people maintain their independence through most, if not all, of their adult life. This exploratory research therefore highlights the experiences and significance of older people living in the private rented sector across diverse geographical areas in Britain.

Current policy links

The research is timely because of the number of relevant policy issues currently under discussion or implementation which relate to older people in private rented housing. These cut across housing, legal and social policy areas, both nationally and locally; they include:

- proposals for better regulation of the private rented sector, including licensing landlords;
- changes to the law on the condition of properties;
- proposals to overhaul the Housing Benefit system;
- the 2002 Homelessness Act, especially the development of homelessness strategies by local authorities;
- changes in the funding of housing and support services (Supporting People);
- the development of the Protection of Vulnerable Adults policies;
- reform of housing law.

These initiatives are set within over-arching national policy frameworks:

- on the need for multi-agency working and joined-up thinking;
- on the health and welfare of older people, including *The National Service Framework for Older People* (DoH, 2001) and *All our futures* (Better Government for Older People Committee, 2000);
- on regulatory reform in all areas of state intervention through the Better Regulation Task Force;
- on the role of the National Care Standards Commission and the merger with the Social Services Inspectorate as a new regulatory framework emerges.

Definitions

For the purposes of this study, 'older people' have been defined as those aged 60 or over, although there is occasional reference to people in their 40s or 50s, who will become the next generation of older people.

A 'common-sense' definition of the 'private rented sector' has been used, namely:

- tenancies of self-contained premises;
- bedsits or rooms in shared houses;
- people with resident landlords/landladies;
- 'Bed & Breakfast' when used as a permanent home.

The research team is aware of a number of issues concerning older people living in 'park homes' (mobile homes where a site rent is paid), and in leasehold properties (generally either purpose-built or converted flats). They are usually owner-occupiers, even though there are limits to their security of tenure, and therefore they were classified as outside the scope of this study.

Research methods

The research team was multi-disciplinary, with academic expertise and professional experience in housing law, legal and housing advice, health and social welfare, and issues relating to older people.

Fieldwork was carried out in six locations in Britain in order to provide a comprehensive and robust

understanding of the processes and issues involved. The following case study locations were chosen on the basis of a combination of contextual factors, including the high proportion of older residents, the nature of the local private rented sector, the nature of the locality (for example, London borough or seaside town) and other information collected during the preparatory work:

- two northern towns
- a city in the midlands
- a city in the south west
- a south coast resort
- a London borough.

In each case study area, semi-structured interviews were conducted with key informants in statutory and voluntary agencies. Agency interviews were evenly spread between voluntary agencies and statutory agencies, with a total of 36 agency staff being interviewed (see the Appendix). Statutory agencies included local authorities' tenancy relations and environmental health departments and the Rent Service. Voluntary agencies included local representatives of national organisations (Shelter and Age Concern), local welfare organisations, housing advisory and homelessness agencies.

Individual interviews and focus groups were also carried out with older private tenants, and with older people who had previously lived in private rented housing but who had been rehoused. Thirty-eight tenant interviews took place in the six localities. There was a good range of tenants, including both couples and single male and female tenants; 11 tenants from minority ethnic communities (four Irish, two Eastern European, four Asian and one African-Caribbean); and an age range from late 40s to 80s, with most in their 60s.

In addition, the research team observed one local authority forum for private landlords, attended by 11 landlords, and interviewed two private landlords, a managing agent and a representative of a local landlord association.

The structure of the report

Chapter 2 explores the development and diversity of the private rented sector, with a particular emphasis on the perspective of older tenants. Chapter 3 goes on to describe the legal framework, and Chapter 4 explores the links between harassment, elder abuse and adult protection. The next four chapters draw directly on the fieldwork. Chapter 5 sets out the experiences of older people with their landlords in private rented housing. Chapter 6 examines the private rented sector as it affects older people; focussing on the reasons older people live in the private rented sector and the impact of the wider housing market. Chapter 7 considers systemic problems, particularly the problems of the Housing Benefit system and the difficulties of using legal remedies to combat harassment. Chapter 8 develops the theme of how best to support older people living in private rented housing, while respecting their choice as to whether they wish to stay or move to alternative accommodation. It focuses in particular on the role of local authorities and on the need for the voluntary sector (especially advice agencies) to help older people obtain housing and services. Chapter 9 concludes with recommendations for national policy changes and local strategies to assist older private tenants.

2

The development of the private rented sector

Introduction

Older people's housing histories are influenced by a variety of factors, including class, income, inheritance, geographical location, employment and marital status (Heywood et al, 2002). Whether or not people are able, or wish to, access other tenures (especially council housing or owner-occupation) is another important factor.

Some of the older tenants interviewed for this study were still in private rented housing in 2001 due to housing histories dating back to the 1930s, 1940s and 1950s. For this reason this chapter starts with a brief historical overview of changes in housing provision during the 20th century. This is followed by a profile of the private rented sector at the end of the 20th century, with particular regard to information on older tenants.

The decline of the private rented sector 1900-89

At the beginning of the 20th century, around 90% of the population lived in properties rented from a private landlord. In 1909, there were about one million small landlords in the United Kingdom, owning on average 7-8 units of housing (Offer, 1981). The mass of the population did not earn enough to save a deposit for a house. Even middle- and upper-class people, who could have bought if they wished, were content to rent, leaving the responsibility for maintenance to the owner and being free to move home whenever it suited them.

Taking advantage of the shortage of housing during the First World War, private landlords increased rents dramatically. Riots in Scotland and the threat of riots elsewhere led to the passing of the 1915 Increase of Rent and Mortgage Interest (War Restrictions) Act, restricting rents to the levels they were at in August 1914. Other Rent Acts, mainly continuing these controls, were passed in the subsequent decades with any attempts to decontrol being countered by political pressure. Landlords could not increase rents, so there was little incentive to invest and every incentive to sell.

Less than 1 million of the 2.5 million new homes in the private sector built between 1919 and 1939 were for letting; the majority were for owner-occupation by the growing band of 'white collar' workers. In the same period, 1.5 million council houses were built and let to working-class families in secure jobs who could afford the rents. Faced with limits on rents and increasing regulation, many private landlords either sold up or tried to avoid the effects of regulation by devious means. Landlords often sold to their tenants. One million tenanted properties changed hands in this way between the First and Second World War, and the process accelerated during and after the Second World War. By 1951 only approximately 45% of the population were tenants of private landlords, compared with 90% 50 years earlier.

Meanwhile, the clearance of the slums had become one of the nation's major priorities. Private landlords who owned properties in the worst city areas could see 'the writing on the wall'. A total of 341,000 slum properties, mainly owned by private landlords, were cleared in England and Wales between 1930 and 1944. This development was made possible by the provision of government subsidy for the building of replacement housing by local authorities. An even greater assault began after the Second World War. In the 20 years from 1960-80, nearly 2 million houses were demolished (Gibson and Langstaff, 1982, p 31). Under the rules of the 1973 Land Compensation Act, landlord owners of unfit properties received site value only, and this, in run-down areas, could be as little as £1 per property. (It was not until 1989 that compensation at market value was reintroduced for landlords.)

Because of an acute shortage of housing of any kind after both World Wars, action on slum clearance had to be balanced with the need for more homes. This led governments to offer grants for improvements such as the installation of a bathroom or indoor WC. In the years between 1964 and 1996, increasingly generous grants were offered, for repairs as well as for improvements. Private landlords were caught up as a minor part of a programme intended mainly to benefit poorer owner-occupiers.

There was also a desire to improve whole areas, and to improve the housing conditions of private sector tenants. At times in the 1980s and 1990s, it was possible for a landlord to receive a grant of up to 100% of the cost of work on the sole condition that the property continued to be available for letting for five years. Not only did the landlord thereby stand to make considerable gain when the five years were up, but they were able, by reference to the rent tribunal, to charge the tenant an increased rent for the improvements paid for from the public purse. These generous grants represented an element of considerable public subsidy to the private rented sector, but they ended in 1996 with the passing of the Housing Grants, Construction and Regeneration Act. In general, however, the private rented sector continued to decline into the 1980s, reaching an all-time low in 1989 of 8.6% of total housing stock.

Growth and change 1990-2000

Since 1989, however, there has been a slow but steady growth in the private rented sector. Changes in legislation brought in by Conservative governments (the 1988 and 1996 Housing Acts) reduced or removed security of tenure and rent restrictions for new lettings, creating assured and assured shorthold tenancies (see Chapter 3 for a detailed discussion on types of tenancy). Since January 1989, nearly all new private sector tenancies have been insecure assured shortholds at market rents.

Conservative governments of this period also attempted to encourage investment in the private rented sector with various schemes offering tax relief (Business Expansion Scheme, Housing Investment Trusts), although financial institutions have remained reluctant to invest in the sector (Crook and Kemp, 1999). During slumps in the house purchase market (particularly in the early 1990s), individual owners who could not sell became landlords for a while, using the rental income to pay the mortgage. During 1993-94, it was estimated that about one in ten lettings was owned by such 'property slump' landlords (Crook et al, 1995). Developers of sheltered housing for sale also entered the residential letting market when they could not sell, providing a new source of privately rented sheltered housing for people aged 50-55 and over. A more important impetus for expansion of the private rented sector since the mid-1990s has been the increasing availability of buy-to-let mortgages for individual small investors.

At the same time that Conservative governments were encouraging the growth of the private rented sector, they were cutting 'bricks and mortar' investment in public sector rented housing. Housing Benefit was left to 'take the strain' of rising rents, providing a public subsidy to parts of the private rented sector. A total of £1,187 million was paid out for tenants of private landlords in 1989/90. By 1999/00 this had risen nearly five-fold, to £5,161 million (DETR, 2000a, p 92). The 1995 White Paper (DoE, 1995) addressed the issue, saying that subsidy for social housing would be more cost-effective long-term than paying Housing Benefit at market rents. The action that was taken, however, was to penalise the private tenants. Regulations introduced by the government in 1996 established various measures designed to limit public expenditure on Housing

Benefit. Housing Benefit was to be paid at least four weeks in arrears. For young single people rent would be paid only at the rate for a single room in shared housing. For others, there was to be a local reference rent, set by rent officers from the Rent Service. This was to be established by investigating local market rents and establishing norms. If a rent was above the norm, full benefit would not be paid. The legislation implied that tenants must either find the difference themselves, negotiate a lower rent with the landlord, or move to cheaper property.

Research evidence shows that in the period 1993-2000, Housing Benefit payments increased by 24%, but rents increased by 31% (DTLR, 2001a, p 75), with much hardship caused to individual tenants (Peakman, 1998). Of the private tenants whose Housing Benefit was lower than the rent in 1999, 40,000 (30% of the total) asked the landlord to reduce the rent, but this was refused in 65% of cases (DTLR, 2001a, p 76). It was estimated by the government that local reference rents and single room rents would together save £170 million in Housing Benefit (about 2.4% of the total expenditure). This does not seem a very significant saving in proportion to the suffering caused. Land and house prices continue to be very inflated in areas of high housing demand, and these are what determine market rents.

Table 1 compares the supply of new homes in 1975 with 1999, and shows that where councils have stopped building, no one else has rushed in to fill the gap. Housing association figures have also gone down, while the number of new homes for owner-occupation was, oddly enough, just the same as it had been in 1975. Overall 129,000 fewer homes for rent were built. Growth in the housing association (registered social landlord, RSL) sector that has been achieved through Large-Scale Voluntary Transfer

(LSVT) of council housing does not indeed create any new homes. These figures reflect the trend of the last 20 years, the shortfall accumulating year on year, so it is not surprising that private landlords are in a position to charge high rents, particularly in areas of housing shortage.

A tenure of last resort?

During the course of the 20th century, the development of council housing and the availability of mortgage finance for owner-occupation provided more attractive alternative sources of housing than private renting for most of the population.

Private renting was left to house two broad categories of people of all ages:

- those who could not access other sectors;
- those who, for one reason or another, found that private rented housing suited their needs better than accommodation available in other tenures.

Many older people who are still private tenants in the first decade of the new millennium trace their private tenancies back to these two broad categories, either because of their own circumstances or those of their families. Others have become private tenants in recent years after rejecting or failing in other tenures.

The people who became private tenants included:

- *Single or childless people* who stood little chance of obtaining a council tenancy. This problem became worse when the policy of 'housing need' points replaced the simple waiting list. Many of the single older people who are currently tenants of private landlords never had the choice of being a

Table 1: Decline of supply of new houses in the late 20th century

	New house starts: owner-occupation	New house starts: housing association (RSL)	New house starts: council and new town housing	Total new houses for rent started	Total new house starts
1975	130,000	19,000	126,000	145,000	275,000
1999	130,000	16,000	183	16,000	146,000

Note: Figures corrected to nearest 1,000.
Source: Wilcox (2000, p 107)

council tenant, first because of the discrimination in favour of those with children, and later because they were housed, and therefore not in 'housing need' as defined by the local authority.

- *Older people who have led an unsettled way of life* have often ended up in the private rented sector. A much higher proportion of single males lives in furnished lets: most of these would probably be rooms in houses in multiple occupation (HMOs)[1]. At the bottom end of the rented market, there are landlords who offer poor quality housing but do not object to life-styles that have resulted in evictions from council or housing association provision. Among older people, this is particularly true of older drinkers who do not want to change their behaviour, and who can no longer access their traditional accommodation such as night shelters or hostels, now dominated by younger people.
- *Migrants*, especially at the time of large-scale immigration from the Commonwealth in the 1960s and 1970s, but also including people from Ireland and Eastern Europe. Most councils had long waiting lists and had introduced residency qualifications, typically of five years, to give priority to local citizens over newcomers (originally, newcomers from other places in Britain). Unless they could afford to buy, new migrants therefore had no choice but private renting.
- *People whose needs are not met in other sectors*. There have always been people whose life-styles have not fitted into other tenures, and there continue to be people who either choose the private sector or end up in it.
- *Carers* who remained in the family home, who then inherited the private tenancy on the death of the parent or relative. It would be expected from general information on carers that these would be mostly single women.
- *People who could not afford either a mortgage or the rents of the new council housing when they first sought housing.* Neither could they afford the fares from the suburbs (where most new housing was built) to the city centres where they worked.
- *People from upper-class backgrounds 'down on their luck',* who would not have considered living in council housing.

- *Older tenants who have links with their landlord which go beyond the strict landlord–tenant contract;* this is especially likely where there is a long-standing tenancy, particularly with a resident landlord, or where there are kinship, friendship or minority community links between tenant and landlord.

Chapter 6 continues the discussion about why older people live in the private rented sector.

A profile of the private rented sector and its older tenants

The *1999 Survey of English Housing* identified 2.3 million private tenancies: over 10% of all homes (DTLR, 2001a). Thus, although owner-occupation is the dominant tenure (69% nationally), private rented housing can be seen as a significant tenure when compared with council tenancies (15%) and housing association (RSL) tenancies (6%). London has the highest proportion of private rented properties (15%). In London boroughs, 31% of all lone pensioners live in unfurnished and a further 3.9% in furnished privately rented accommodation. It is very important, when general averages are considered, that this particular issue of the size and scale of the problem in London, one which has deep historical roots, is not forgotten (see, for example, Tarn, 1973).

Types of tenancy

Over half of all private tenancies (54%) were assured shorthold tenancies with very little security of tenure. A further 12% were assured tenancies. All these tenancies (two thirds of the total) have been created since 1989 under the 1988 Housing Act. Of the remaining third of private tenancies, 19% were classified as 'not accessible to the public', being either within families or 'tied' to employment, and about half of these were rent-free. Eight per cent had no security, usually because there was a resident landlord. Seven per cent were the old regulated or protected tenancies created before 1989 under the 1977 Rent Act.

Table 2: Percentages of different age ranges in the private rented sector

Age group	Private tenants receiving Housing Benefit	Private tenants not receiving Housing Benefit	All private tenants
16-24	11	26	22
25-39	44	50	49
40-59	22	15	17
60 and over	23	8	12
All age groups	100	100	100

Source: DLTR (2001a)

As Table 2 shows, currently, just 12% of all private rented sector tenants are aged 60 and over and 70% are aged under 45. The new, commercial private rented sector has become a tenure mainly for the young employed, who will generally have assured shorthold tenancies.

It is quite different for regulated tenancies. Since no new tenancies of this kind have been possible since 1989, the proportion of older people is much higher. Fifty-four per cent of regulated tenancies housed a single adult aged over 60, and 23% housed two adults aged over 60. The distinction between assured and regulated tenancies is crucial in this study (see Chapter 3).

Twenty-three per cent of all private tenancies comprise a single male living alone and 15% a single woman (DTLR, 2001, p 13). Among all the older households in Britain, single older households are over-represented in the private rented sector (Table 3).

Table 3: Percentage of private renting by household type (households headed by a person aged 60 or more), England (1995)

	Private unfurnished renting	Private furnished renting
Single male	14	40
Single female	41	23
Couple, one 60+	12	9
Other two person	26	9
Other	9	20
All households	100	100

Source: ONS (1996)

Disrepair and lack of facilities

Although private tenants are less likely than council tenants to complain about the state of repair of their home (DTLR, 2001a), the private rented sector has much higher levels of unfitness and disrepair than other sectors. This is especially true among regulated tenancies and the lack of complaints may be as much to do with tenants' expectations as the actual condition of their property or the fear of eviction or harassment.

The *1996 English House Condition Survey* (DETR, 1996) showed that the private rented sector was between three and four times worse than other sectors for the proportion of dwellings which failed the fitness standard (the current measure of house condition), as shown in Table 4. The most common reason for unfitness in general related to unsatisfactory conditions for preparation and cooking of food. Other reasons included disrepair, dampness, lack of facilities and lack of means of escape from fire.

Table 4: Proportion of dwellings failing to meet the fitness standard on at least one measure

Tenure	Proportion of unfit dwellings
Private rented sector	19.3
Local authority	7.3
Owner-occupied	6.0
Registered Social Landlords	5.2
All tenures	7.5

Note: The fitness standard is defined under Section 604 of the 1985 Housing Act as recast by the 1989 Local Government and Housing Act, Schedule 9, paragraph 83. Since 1996 plans have been underway to introduce a wholly new way of assessing unfitness, based on risk assessment.

Source: DETR (1998) *1996 English House Condition Survey*

The level of 'unfitness' in the private rented sector is partly due to the age of housing stock in the sector: about half the stock is older than 75 years. Between the housing condition surveys of 1991 and 1996 there was no overall reduction in the proportion of the nation's housing stock that was unfit.

The private rented housing which older people on low income are able to afford is often in a much poorer condition than average rented housing. The higher rate of unfitness for habitation is experienced more by older people living alone than by those in couples or other types of household. Rates of unfitness experienced by female-headed households in the older age groups are also generally higher than for households headed by men. Older men living alone are more likely to live in unfit dwellings than older women living alone; this would link with the number in bedsits and rooms in HMOs (DoE, 1993).

The highest incidence of unfitness and poor conditions is in 'traditional' HMOs: large properties divided into furnished bedsits with shared kitchens and bathrooms. Almost two thirds of these 'traditional' HMOs failed, most commonly due to lack of adequate means of escape from fire, with 40% having unsatisfactory kitchen areas and/or enough sanitary facilities. The larger the HMO, the poorer the conditions tended to be.

Rents and deposits

The average rent in England in 1999 for a private sector tenancy, after deducting water rates and including any Housing Benefit, was £86 per week. There was a marked difference in the average for regulated tenancies which generally have 'fair' rents registered by the Rent Service (£52 per week) and the average for assured shorthold tenancies (£94 per week). There were also significant regional differences, from £61 per week in the West Midlands to £131 per week in London in 1999 (DTLR, 2001a). Seventy-one per cent of all those who had started a tenancy in the previous five years had been required to pay a deposit: on average £450. About 26% of all private tenants (but 47% of regulated tenants) receive Housing Benefit, at an average rate in 1999 of £63 per week. This average figure masks the high rates of Housing Benefit being paid in areas of high rents.

Who are the landlords?

As set out in the historical overview (see earlier), landlords will have entered the market at different times and for different reasons. There is a wide variation in types of landlord, as well as in the size and condition of the housing they provide. Crook et al (1995) found that 57% of private rented dwellings were owned by private individuals and couples, often referred to as 'amateur' landlords. A further 25% were owned by partnerships or companies. The remaining 18% of dwellings were owned by a mixture of organisations which are classified as part of the private rented sector, although they do not fit most people's idea of a 'private landlord' and include quasi-public bodies, such as charities and trusts (for example, the National Trust), the Church and Crown Commissioners, and government departments.

Table 5 shows that in 1993-94, over a quarter of all landlords (26%) owned only one dwelling and a further 29% owned between 2 and 9 dwellings. It can be assumed that these are the 'amateur' landlords, while the larger property portfolios would belong to the property companies and the other organisations listed above. Investors are said to be wary of the sector because there are not enough sufficiently large companies running it (Crook and Kemp, 1999).

Research published in Birmingham in 1995 (Trickett, 1995) revealed that the average number of properties owned by the 44 landlords in the survey was 9 (range: 2-69). The owners who were mainly small-scale capitalists, had identified niche markets for

Table 5: Size of English landlord's lettings portfolio (1993/94)

Number of lettings	%
1	26
2-4	17
5-9	12
10-24	14
25-49	7
50-99	5
100-249	6
250-499	3
500-999	2
1,000+	7
Total	100
(Base)	(527)

Note: Figures do not total 100 due to rounding.
Source: Crook and Kemp (1996)

themselves and preferred to let to one specific tenant group. Few of the landlords were interested in expanding their business, and some claimed that they let properties as much as a social service as for profit, or that they wanted to get out of the business. Widespread ignorance of the law was found, particularly in relation to possession procedures and landlord and tenant legislation (Trickett, 1995). The research also looked at the portfolios of properties (from 11 to 2,500) managed by letting or managing agents. These showed a volatile market almost entirely concerned with lettings to more prosperous tenants and not generally designed for long-term occupation.

Summary

The historical overview and the profile of the private rented sector sets the scene for this study. There are a number of key characteristics when considering the position of older people as private sector tenants:

- A wide variety of life course factors as well as the housing market issues of the last 60 years have led people to end up as older tenants in the private rented sector.
- In particular, discrimination by social landlords against childless people, and transitory life-styles have all barred access to other tenures, especially for single people.
- Nationally, most tenants in the private rented sector are now younger people: in 1999, 70% were under 45 and only 12% were aged 60 and over.
- In the regulated tenancy private sector, however, 77% of the tenancies house people aged 60 and over.
- Older private tenants are more likely than younger tenants to be living in properties which are in poor condition or lacking facilities, and if they are regulated tenants, to be paying lower than average rents.
- Many older people will have been living in their private rented housing for decades, because all regulated tenancies will have started before 1989, whereas many younger people use the private rented sector for short-term accommodation.
- In London, there is a larger than average proportion of older single people living in the private rented sector.

Note

[1] A house that was originally built as a single family residence but which has now been divided into multiple residences for more than one household or individuals living separately.

3

Legal protection, legal remedies and the private rented sector

Introduction

This chapter explains the different forms of housing tenure, and, in particular, the effect this has on security of tenure and protection from eviction. It defines harassment and illegal eviction, and sets out the legal remedies available. It also summarises the actions which can be taken by both tenants and local authorities to tackle disrepair, and explains the legal position on rent increases.

Occupational status and security of tenure

For many people living in rented accommodation, one of their worst fears is being evicted from their homes. How easy it is in practice for landlords to evict them (the extent of their 'security of tenure') depends on whether they are a tenant or a licensee, and on what kind of tenancy or licence they have been given. The legal rights of occupants will vary according to this 'occupational status'[1]. In most cases occupational status will be clear-cut, but sometimes it can be difficult to determine whether someone was given a tenancy or a licence. The distinction between the two, however, is very important: tenants have the right to refuse entry to their landlords (except in very limited circumstances, see below), whereas licensees do not. In this section the various types of occupational status commonly found in the private rented sector will be summarised and the security of tenure attached to them will be discussed.

A *tenancy* is an 'estate in land' and is similar to owner-occupation in some respects – the tenant has the right to control who comes and goes in the property. A tenant can exclude anyone from his/her home, including the landlord. Landlords often do not realise that their tenants have this right; they think that because they own the property, they must be able to let themselves in and out as they see fit. Tenants can, if they choose, change the locks on their doors and are not obliged to let their landlords have a key. The only right of entry landlords have is to view the property for disrepair and to carry out repairs, after first giving their tenants at least 24 hours' notice in writing (1985 Landlord and Tenant Act, Section 11.6).

By contrast, a *licence* is merely a permission to occupy the premises. The landlord retains control of the property and can decide who comes and goes. The landlord exercises unrestricted access to the accommodation. If, for example, the licence relates to a room in a hotel or hostel, the owner/manager of the building can ask the licensee to change rooms by giving reasonable notice. Licences may also be given where the landlord requires entry to fulfil the terms of the licence agreement, such as where cleaning or other forms of support are provided, as in some types of supported housing.

The law affords varying degrees of protection from eviction to both tenants and licensees. However, it must be remembered that landlords do not always abide by the law, and tenants do not always seek advice to enable them to enforce their rights.

In most cases, landlords must obtain a court order for possession before the occupant can be evicted, and it is a criminal offence if they do not do so (1977 Protection from Eviction Act, Section 1). Once the court has sanctioned eviction, the landlord must ask the court bailiff to carry out the eviction. This process can take several weeks, and most cases of illegal eviction occur because the landlord does not want to have to wait that long or incur legal expenses.

The only exceptions to the requirement of obtaining a court order before eviction are six instances set out in the 1977 Protection from Eviction Act, Section 3A, which defines *excluded tenancies and excluded licences*. The most common type of excluded tenancy or licence is where the occupant is sharing essential living accommodation (a living room, kitchen or bathroom) with a resident landlord (who could either be an owner-occupier or a tenant). Occupants of night shelters are also excluded licensees, and tenants/licensees who do not pay any rent are also in the excluded categories.

Most occupants in the private rented sector are, however, tenants. There are two broad categories of tenants:

- *regulated or protected tenants* under the 1977 Rent Act (the terms are interchangeable and this report will use the term 'regulated tenant');
- *assured tenants* and *assured shorthold tenants* under the 1988 Housing Act.

Which Act applies depends on when the tenancy began. Most tenancies that were created prior to 15 January 1989 were regulated tenancies under the 1977 Rent Act. Those created on or after that date will generally be assured shorthold tenancies (mainly in the private rented sector) or assured tenancies (mainly in housing association properties).

Regulated tenants under the 1977 Rent Act have a considerable degree of security of tenure. Before they can be evicted, the landlord must properly end the contract for the tenancy and then obtain a court order for possession. In order to obtain a court order, the landlord has to prove one of 20 grounds for possession. Some of the grounds are mandatory grounds, and the court *must* grant a court order if the ground is proven. Others are discretionary grounds for possession, in which case the court has to be satisfied that it is reasonable to evict the tenant, given all of the circumstances of the case, even if the ground is proved. Rent arrears is the ground for

possession most commonly used, and it is discretionary. Consequently, even if a tenant is in rent arrears, the court may not order eviction if there is some reasonable explanation given of why the tenant is in arrears.

Another important characteristic of regulated tenancies is that tenants can apply for a 'fair rent' to be registered by the rent officer. Rents are fixed according to a statutory formula, and once registered, they can be increased only every two years. It is illegal to charge more than the registered rent, and tenants can reclaim overpaid rent for a period of up to two years. This means that the landlord does not have control of the rent level, which makes this form of tenancy very unpopular with landlords.

The other important characteristic of regulated tenancies of relevance to this study is the right of a spouse and/or family member to succeed the tenancy on the death of the tenant. This statutory right allows first a spouse and then any member of the family to succeed to (take over) the tenancy when the tenant dies. A spouse will continue to have a regulated tenancy. For a family member to succeed, he or she must have been living with the tenant for two years prior to the tenant's death. When a family member succeeds the tenancy, it is converted automatically into an assured tenancy. In this way the government ensured that regulated tenancies would eventually be phased out. The 1988 Housing Act did not give rights of succession to family members of assured and assured shorthold tenancies, although spouses or cohabitants can succeed to the tenancy. During the fieldwork we came across a number of difficult cases with problems over succession, as discussed in Chapter 5. The extensive rights of succession to regulated tenancies are another reason why they were unpopular with landlords.

Private sector tenancies created on or after 15 January 1989 are generally covered by the 1988 Housing Act. This Act made two important changes to private tenancies:

- it removed rent control and substituted market rents;
- it introduced a new form of tenancy that has very little security of tenure, the assured shorthold tenancy.

After that date, no new regulated tenancies could be created, although existing Rent Act tenancies continued in existence and were generally unaffected by the later Act. This means that the number of Rent Act tenancies is gradually dwindling as regulated tenants either die or move out.

As noted above, tenancies under the 1988 Housing Act will either be assured or assured shorthold tenancies. Assured tenancies have a fairly good degree of security. Before the tenant can be evicted, the landlord must obtain a court order for possession by proving a ground for possession, which will either be mandatory or discretionary, as in the 1977 Rent Act. However, the grounds for possession under the later Act are rather different from Rent Act grounds. In particular, the 1988 Act created a mandatory ground for possession based on two months' rent arrears. Consequently, the court will have to order eviction if the tenant is more than two months in arrears, regardless of the reasons those arrears arose.

An assured shorthold tenancy is a form of assured tenancy with an extra ground for possession, the shorthold ground, which is mandatory. This means that if the landlord follows the correct procedures, a shorthold tenant can be evicted easily, without the need even to attend a court hearing. A landlord can obtain a possession order by simply proving that the tenancy was a shorthold tenancy, and that the correct notice was given prior to commencing possession proceedings. No other factors are relevant, and the court cannot take into account any of the surrounding circumstances. Landlords cannot obtain possession using the shorthold ground during the first six months of the tenancy, but after that the tenant has very little security.

When the 1988 Housing Act first became effective on 15 January 1989, landlords had to give a written notice that they intended to give a shorthold tenancy and had to create a fixed term tenancy of at least six months' duration. If they failed to follow the requirements of the Act, they created an assured tenancy by default. That position was reversed by the 1996 Housing Act. For tenancies that were created on or after 28 February 1997, the landlord has to give notice in writing that s/he is creating an assured tenancy. All other tenancies are shorthold by default. So, assured shorthold tenancies no longer have to be given for a fixed term, nor do they have to be created by a written contract. They can be created by an oral contract.

In summary, 1977 Rent Act tenants have a very secure form of occupation. The grounds for possession which the landlord must prove before the court will order eviction means that in practice it can be quite difficult for a landlord to regain possession of the property. Since January 1989, however, most private tenants were given assured shorthold tenancies, which generally offer good protection from eviction only during the first six months of the tenancy, after which it is relatively easy to obtain a court order for possession. If assured or assured shorthold tenants have rent arrears amounting to more than eight weeks/two months rent, the landlord can claim possession of the dwelling using a mandatory ground for possession, and the court will have to evict the tenant.

Some occupants, notably those who share essential living accommodation with resident landlords (excluded tenants or licensees), have no protection from eviction whatsoever. Their landlords do not have go to court, nor do they have to give written notice before evicting the occupant. The occupants are entitled only to reasonable or contractual notice, after which they become trespassers. Their landlords can then use reasonable force to remove them from the premises without having to obtain the court's permission.

Proposals to reform housing law

The Law Commission has just consulted on proposals for the reform and simplification of housing law in relation to housing status and security of tenure[2]. If adopted, these proposals would result in the creation of two basic types of housing agreements (referred to as Type I and Type II agreements). The importance of the distinction between tenancies and licences would also be reduced, because most licensees (apart from those currently in the 'excluded categories' under the 1977 Protection from Eviction Act) would have the same legal protection afforded to tenants. Type I agreements would replace those currently given by local authorities and RSLs (secure tenancies under the 1985 Housing Act and assured tenancies under the 1988 Housing Act). Existing regulated tenancies under the 1977 Rent Act would also be converted into Type I agreements, with separate legislation brought in to protect regulated tenants' right to register a 'fair rent'. Type II agreements are modelled on the current assured shorthold tenancy, and would include both fixed-term and periodic agreements.

As a result of the proposed reforms, housing agreements would be controlled by consumer protection legislation, rather than by property law, as is now the case. There would be a requirement for landlords to give written agreements, as the contract would become the key element in the landlord–tenant relationship. The contract would have to provide a statement of both parties' rights and obligations, including the grounds for possession. Type I agreements will not be permitted to contain mandatory grounds for possession; the court would always have a discretion as to whether to grant an order for possession. Type II agreements would contain both discretionary and mandatory grounds, including the equivalent of a shorthold ground for possession and a mandatory ground for possession on the basis of eight weeks' or two months' rent arrears.

Although it is suggested that RSLs might be allowed to issue Type II agreements in certain circumstances, the Consultation Paper (Law Commission, 2002) assumes that this form of agreement, which offers a reduced level of security, would be used mainly by private sector landlords. It also assumes that longer-term security of tenure would only be offered by social landlords, unless private landlords for some reason choose to use Type I agreements.

Legal definitions of harassment and unlawful eviction

The term 'harassment' has not been defined as such in law, probably in order to give as much leeway as possible to the courts when they are asked to deal with behaviour that can be said to amount to harassment. Consequently, there are a number of torts (civil wrongs) and criminal offences that relate to behaviour which would amount to abuse and harassment. A few examples are set out below:

- Harassment under the 1997 Protection from Harassment Act, Section 1 ('PHA 97'), which is both a tort and a criminal offence under that Act. (See below for a further discussion of harassment under this Act.)

- Putting someone in fear of violence on at least two occasions, which is a criminal offence under the 1997 Protection from Harassment Act, Section 4.

- Nuisance, a tort which is defined as interference with reasonable use or enjoyment of land. The interference must emanate from neighbouring land or property. Examples would be excessive noise or disturbance from an adjoining flat or house, or smells, which must be judged against the standards of the average person.

- Trespass to land, a tort which is defined as unlawful interference with land. Once premises are let to a tenant, the tenant has control over who can and cannot enter the premises, including the landlord (except to view for repairs). If the landlord or her/his agent goes into the premises without the tenant's permission, s/he will be trespassing on the property. Similarly, unlawfully placing something on the tenant's premises will be a trespass.

- Forcing entry into premises by using violence or threats, when there is someone present who is opposed to the entry, is a criminal offence if the person forcing entry knows that is the case (1977 Criminal Law Act, Section 6).

- Trespass to goods, a tort defined as a direct interference with another person's belongings. Examples would range from moving or removing someone's belongings unlawfully to damaging or destroying or stealing goods.

- Intimidation, in the context of the law of tort, which is defined as any threat, whether by words or actions, which is intended to make someone do something that causes damage to that person or to someone else. The threat must be such as to coerce, rather than persuade, someone and must be accompanied by a demand. It must also be a threat to do something unlawful. An example would be, "Get out by the end of the week or I'll kick you out". Because the threat would amount to an illegal eviction, it constitutes intimidation.

- 1988 Housing Act, Section 27, creates a tort which consists of unlawfully depriving or attempting to deprive a residential occupier (tenant or licensee) of all or part of the premises. It also consists of doing acts calculated to interfere with the peace or comfort of the occupier and/or members of the household or withholding services reasonably required for the occupation of the premises, so long as it is done intentionally in order to make the occupier give up occupation or refrain from exercising a right or pursuing a remedy. Similar behaviour is also a crime under the 1977 Protection from Eviction Act, as amended by the 1988 Housing Act.

'Harassment' is not defined in detail under the 1997 Protection from Harassment Act, but under the terms of that Act it is seen as including alarming or causing a person distress. A Law Commission report (1992, para 3.1) on domestic violence listed a number of examples of acts which have been held (in the context of domestic violence) to amount to harassment or molestation:

- persistent pestering and intimidation through shouting, denigration, threats or argument;
- nuisance telephone calls;
- damaging property;
- writing anonymous letters;
- pressing one's face against a window while brandishing papers.

The most important factor in all of these actions is the effect of the behaviour on the victim and the perpetrator's intentions in committing them. Some actions will be intrinsically threatening or damaging, but even seemingly innocuous actions become threatening when repeated over and over or when carried out in the context of previous menaces or violence.

In addition to the above torts and criminal offences, harassment and abuse would amount to a breach of contract between landlord and tenant. Every tenancy agreement, whether oral or in writing, contains a covenant by the landlord to allow the tenant 'quiet enjoyment' of the premises. The meaning of this phrase has been broadly interpreted, and breaches of the covenant would include any form of disturbance, regardless of whether there has been direct physical interference with possession of the premises or the tenant's possessions. Examples include letters threatening eviction together with going to the premises and knocking on the door and shouting threats. Another example would be cutting off gas or electricity. Serious disrepair can also constitute a breach.

In this study, we have considered 'abuse and harassment' to be any behaviour that would give the victim the right to take civil proceedings, or for which the perpetrator could be prosecuted. The most wide-ranging connotations of harassment of all those set out above would be those used in the 1997 Protection from Harassment Act ("causing alarm or distress") and in breaches of the covenant of quiet enjoyment ("any form of disturbance").

Legal remedies for harassment and illegal eviction

Civil law provides a number of legal remedies for most people who have been the victims of harassment and/or illegal eviction. Tenants and licensees who have been illegally evicted can sue for breach of contract to obtain damages (compensation) and an order reinstating them to the property (apart from those in the 'excluded categories' discussed above). Tenants can also sue if they have been subjected to the torts of trespass to land and nuisance. Anyone can sue if their goods have been unlawfully interfered with, or if they have been the victims of the torts of harassment, intimidation, assault and/or battery. In such cases applications can be made to court for the perpetrator to pay damages, and for a court order to prevent further unlawful behaviour (injunctions). Breach of a civil court order is punishable by an unlimited fine or imprisonment for up to two years (although this rarely happens in practice). However, Chapter 7 will discuss how difficult it actually is for older tenants to use these powers.

Local authorities can prosecute the offences of illegal eviction and harassment defined in the 1977 Protection from Eviction Act; as a matter of policy the police do not do so. However, local authorities have no powers of arrest for these offences. Local authorities do not have a duty to prosecute for illegal eviction, but Marsh et al (2000) take the view that they have a duty to at least consider whether to do so. Action taken by local authorities varies widely, and there appears to be some confusion among tenancy relations officers about what their powers and duties are in relation to cases of illegal eviction and harassment.

The police can prosecute offences under the 1997 Protection from Harassment, as can local authorities under their general powers. The criminal courts have the power to make restraining orders under the Act, which are similar to injunctions and provide the victim with continuing protection from harassment once the proceedings are over. Breach of a civil court injunction order made under the Act is a criminal offence, and the police can prosecute in such cases. Only the police can prosecute offences under the 1977 Criminal Law Act (using violence or threats to enter premises where there is someone present who is opposed to the entry). Again, Chapter 7 will outline why it is difficult to take advantage of these legal options.

Finally, the law generally affords good legal remedies to tenants if their landlords fail to repair their premises. Licensees have less protection, unless they are injured or suffer damage to their personal belongings. In appropriate cases tenants and licensees can make applications to court for compensation. Tenants can apply for a court order to make their landlords carry out the required repairs. Both tenants and licensees can in some cases obtain injunctions to prevent further harm from taking place. However, in reality, the same barriers to obtaining legal redress exist in these cases as with the other remedies discussed above (see Chapter 7).

Local authority powers

Local authorities have considerable powers to control poor housing conditions under the 1985 Housing Act and the 1990 Environmental Protection Act, but whether they use them depends on available resources and local priorities.

Environmental health law covers all residential property, regardless of tenure, but, as discussed in Chapter 2, private rented housing has traditionally had the highest levels of disrepair. For example, in one of the case study localities, a house condition survey had indicated that private rented housing was three times as likely to be unfit or in disrepair as other tenures. There is specific legislation allowing local authorities to take steps to license, control and even manage HMOs, but its use has been patchy.

Local authorities have a duty to investigate complaints about disrepair and poor conditions if brought to their attention, but within clear legal boundaries. At various times during the 20th century there have been initiatives to deal with particular concentrations of poor housing, ranging from slum clearance to area improvement. Local authorities are required to review the housing needs of their areas periodically (1985 Housing Act, Section 8). As part of that, they must, at least once a year, consider the condition of all the housing in their areas, irrespective of tenure (1985 Housing Act, Section 605; DoE, 1996). Older tenants are particularly reluctant to complain, even if their housing conditions are very poor.

From the mid-19th century to the 1990s, the emphasis was on assessing 'fitness'. This included amenities (for example, inside WC, washbasin) and structural items (for example, freedom from damp or leaking roofs). The government is currently consulting on major changes to housing standards which will be much more flexible and are especially relevant to older people. The new Housing Health and Safety Rating System will shift the emphasis from amenities and structure to a risk assessment approach. This is likely to benefit older people because problems such as steep stairs or poor internal layouts will have to be taken into account.

Rent increases: what legal protection do tenants have?

One of the main concerns expressed during the fieldwork was the fear of rent increases which older people could not afford. In theory, rent increases would be covered by Housing Benefit, but this is not true in all cases, and many older people are either too proud to claim means-tested benefits, or fall just above the entitlement level because of savings or a small occupational pension.

As discussed in Chapter 2, there is no effective protection against rent increases for assured or assured shorthold tenants, nor for licensees, since such rents are expected to be set at market levels. Although an assured or assured shorthold tenant can in theory ask the Rent Assessment Committee to reduce their rent, such a course of action is never proposed by housing advisers due to the very great risk that instead of a reduction, the rent will be increased.

The position is quite different for regulated tenants since their rents are still controlled under the 1977 Rent Act, as referred to above. Most regulated tenants are older people. However, over recent years there have been major problems due to the effect of legal challenges to limits on fair rents during 1999 and 2000 (referred to as the Spath Holme case[3]). Although now resolved, it caused two years of confusion, a great deal of worry for older tenants who were affected, and an enormous amount of work for rent officers, advice agencies and indeed for landlords. It is also important to mention because of the percentage limits (albeit above inflation) which are now set on fair rent increases.

In summary, the government introduced the Maximum Fair Rent Order on 1 February 1999. 'Fair rents' have always been calculated by the rent officer on the basis of the market rent, less the 'scarcity' factor, and other disregards for services (such as heating and hot water). However, in the 1990s, there were some large increases in fair rents which then had a knock-on effect on the cost of Housing Benefit. Perhaps not surprisingly, the Conservative government did not appear too concerned about this effect of 'the market', despite its effect on public expenditure: rent controls would have been anathema to them.

However, the Labour government decided to take action and introduced the Order which limited rent increases by linking them to increases in the Retail Price Index (RPI) plus a set percentage. From the date of the Order, the Maximum Fair Rent was the existing registered rent, plus the percentage change in the RPI, and a further 7.5% (if the first re-registration) or 5% (for subsequent re-registrations). There is no limit if it is the first time the rent has been registered, or if landlord repairs and improvements lead to a new fair rent which is over 15% above the previous registered fair rent. This gave landlords an incentive to improve their property to escape the rent limit, which sounds a good thing, except that many older tenants do not want the disruption of works, nor the subsequent rent increase. Pressure to allow improvements to be done can even be a form of harassment, used to 'encourage' older regulated tenants to leave.

A large property company, Spath Holme Ltd, challenged the legality of the Order in the courts. The Court of Appeal held it to be illegal and quashed it on 20 January 2000. However, the House of Lords overturned the Court of Appeal decision on 7 December 2000.

This meant that fair rents set during most of 2000 were not subject to the percentage limits but, once the Lords overturned the Court of Appeal decision, they had to be reassessed according to the percentage limit, also causing problems for Housing Benefit payments.

Summary

In theory, regulated tenancies provide good protection from eviction. There is also a wide range of remedies available for harassment, under both civil and criminal law. In contrast, assured shorthold tenants and licensees have very little protection against eviction and some (especially tenants with resident landlords) have no security whatsoever. This makes them less able to pursue other legal remedies (such as for harassment or disrepair) for fear of retaliatory eviction.

Since protection from eviction is also important with regard to pursuing other actions, it might therefore be thought that older people who are regulated tenants would be in a strong position. However, most tenants (of any age) find it difficult, stressful and potentially too expensive to pursue legal remedies and this is especially true of older people. Without help from housing or legal advice agencies, many older tenants are unable to enforce their rights under housing law. For non-regulated tenants these rights are also very limited.

Local authorities do not always use their legal powers to deal with poor housing conditions because of resource and time constraints, and generally prefer to adopt a negotiating stance in all but the worst cases, as discussed further in Chapter 8. There are effectively no controls on most rent levels, although there are percentage increase limits on 'fair rents' (albeit above RPI) for regulated tenancies.

Notes

[1] Occupational status is not what they do for a living, but the legal term for the basis on which they occupy a property.

[2] Law Commission (2002); also available at www.lawcom.gov.uk.

[3] *R v Secretary of State for the Environment, Transport and Regions and Another, ex parte Spath Holme Ltd* (2000) UKHL 61; (2001) 1 All ER 195.

4

Elder abuse and adult protection: definitions and debates

There are two approaches to supporting older private tenants who have difficulties in their housing. The first is through various aspects of housing law, including housing and benefits advice, tenancy support and environmental health action. The second potential approach is through steps to deal with elder abuse, and adult protection policies.

This chapter explores the relevance of the latter approach to older tenants living in the private rented sector who may be harassed or abused. It then explores the relevance for older private tenants of recent initiatives to develop vulnerable adult policies.

Action on Elder Abuse (cited in McCreadie, 1996, pp 9-12) defines abuse as "a single or repeated act or lack of appropriate action occurring within any relationship where there is an expectation of trust which causes harm or distress to an older person".

Action on Elder Abuse (2002) recognises five main types of abuse:

- *physical* – for example, hitting, slapping, burning, pushing, restraining, or giving too much medication or the wrong medication;
- *psychological* – for example, shouting, swearing, frightening, blaming, ignoring or humiliating a person;
- *financial* – for example, the illegal or unauthorised use of a person's property, money, pension book or other valuable;
- *sexual* – for example, forcing a person to take part in any sexual activity without his or her consent; this can occur within any relationship;

- *neglect* – for example, where a person is deprived of food, heat, clothing, comfort or essential medication.

There have been numerous other attempts to define elder abuse (for example, Eastman, 1984; SSI, 1993) with definitions varying, depending on who is defining the problem: victim, carer, physician, nurse, social worker and so on (Glendenning, 1993). Only one identified definition was found to include housing: Lau and Kosberg (1979) include violation of rights, such as being forced out of one's dwelling, or forced into another setting.

Over the years there has been great variation in what is included or excluded from the definitions and this is closely linked to the fact that elder abuse has no legal meaning (Ashton, 1994). Under such circumstances it is not surprising that the most comprehensive review of the elder abuse literature (McCreadie, 1996) suggests that such research rarely discusses where people live and hardly ever mentions tenure.

There are a number of reasons for this situation. First, the concept of elder abuse was developed by small groups of health and social care professionals (Biggs et al, 1995), rather than older people themselves. Housing professionals were not involved and tenure was not considered.

Official concern with abuse of vulnerable adults has been expressed mainly in the regulation of residential care and nursing homes. It is only recently that concern has spread wider, with the publication of government guidance in *No secrets* (DoH, 2000a), which stressed the need for a multi-agency approach at the local level (discussed further in Chapter 8). There is still concern that this guidance does not pay sufficient attention to preventative work in the community (Slater, 2001). This is despite the acknowledged importance of social inclusion and meaningful occupation as factors in active ageing and emotional and physical health and well-being, as set out in a whole range of government publications (see, for example, DoH, 1998, 2000b, 2001).

There are strong suggestions that abuse is more likely to take place when older people are isolated (Pillemer, 1996; Anderson, 1999), and isolation is an issue for many older people in private tenancies. As discussed in Chapter 2, many older private tenants have always been single, and in older age they are likely to have lost many or all of the relatives and friends they had when younger. Yet research has shown that older people rely on relatives and friends for information, preferring to turn to them if there is no obvious information source (Tinker et al, 1993).

Second, elder abuse debates have focused mainly on care within the domestic home setting or institutions, and on relationships between older people and their informal and formal carers. There is no discussion of the relationship between tenant and landlord and only an occasional mention of abuse by strangers. The most recent prevalence study (Pritchard, 2000) confirmed previous findings: of 126 reported cases, 107 were living in 'domestic settings' rather than care homes, but out of the 98 identified abusers, the majority (77) were relatives, the others being staff, neighbours and friends. Only three were strangers and none was identified as a landlord. However, such findings need to be treated with great caution since what is found tends to be heavily influenced by how elder abuse is defined for research purposes.

An analysis of calls to Action on Elder Abuse's confidential national telephone helpline (Jenkins et al, 2000) drew from 1,421 calls identifying reported incidents of elder abuse and recorded over two years between 1997 and 1999. Two thirds of all calls were about abuse in people's own homes, although tenure was not identified, and just over a quarter about abuse in hospital, residential or nursing care.

Those identified as abusers were predominantly relatives (46%) or paid workers (29.4%). A total of 165 reported abusers (10%) were classified as 'other':

this category included 'a wide variety of people who had access to vulnerable older people such as accountants, wardens, workmen, ancillary staff in residential homes, fellow residents, landlords and lodgers'. There is no further information on how many of this number were landlords: it may be assumed that there would only be a handful, given the large number of categories included as 'other'.

Third, there is a debate within the abuse literature as to whether older people should be considered as an homogenous group or remain undifferentiated from other adults. There appear to be two perspectives. In one view, abuse is constructed by age and/or gender (for example, child abuse, domestic violence). The other view considers that any adult over the age of 18 years can be subject to abuse if they are 'vulnerable'. Vulnerability can stem from age (for example, 'elderly and frail') or from other causes (for example, physical or learning disabilities). However, commentators point out that there are major difficulties in linking protection for all vulnerable adults, since older people "are in the main considered as autonomous adults afforded the same freedoms and citizenship as any other adult" (Bennett et al, 1997, p 25).

For many years there have been calls for legislation to protect vulnerable adults of any age, and draft adult protection legislation has been outlined for consultation (Lord Chancellor's Department, 1997, 1999). However, legislation is not now proposed and the most recent report (Lord Chancellor's Department, 1999) stated that there would be no new offence to mistreat or neglect a vulnerable adult. The preferred approach is the policy framework set out in *No secrets* (DoH, 2000a).

Exploring differences between emotional and contractual relationships

The Action on Elder Abuse definition of abuse broadens the range of perpetrators from carers to anyone in a relationship of trust. However, it is questionable as to how far the Action on Elder Abuse definition was ever intended to cover a relationship such as that between landlord and tenant when it is primarily a legal contract.

There is a diversity of relationships between landlord and tenant. These range from an absentee landlord, who has never met the tenant, to situations where landlord (male or female) and tenant have a closer link than the formal contract of the tenancy, as with some of the older tenants described in Chapter 5. Examples of such intimacy might include:

- resident landlord and one or more tenants who have shared a building (and sometimes facilities such as kitchen or bathroom), perhaps for a long time, and developed friendships or informal carer relationships (these can be landlord caring for tenant, or tenant caring for landlord);
- resident or non-resident landlord and tenant who share ethnic, religious or cultural links, especially within minority ethnic communities;
- landlord–tenant relationships linked to current or previous employment (especially if long-standing);
- landlord–tenant relationships where there is a family relationship.

There are also situations, particularly in shared houses, Bed & Breakfasts or HMOs where the landlord/landlady is undertaking a formal role which does include an element of care and support.

Where there are either emotional ties or an element of care and support, there is considerable scope for abuse as well as harassment. The elder abuse literature and strategies are likely to be more relevant in cases where the relationship between landlord and tenant goes beyond the formal legal contract. Housing law and remedies on harassment are likely to be more appropriate where the relationship is restricted to the landlord–tenant contract.

There are some links between the literature on elder abuse and the position of older tenants in private rented housing. Penhale (1993) notes some of the barriers to reporting elder abuse, and Table 6 demonstrates how the same issues could apply to many older tenants in the private rented sector.

The Social Services Inspectorate (1993) defines abuse as a violation of personal boundaries and disregard of key values: autonomy, respect, participation, knowledge, fulfillment, privacy and equality. Similar values underpin *The National Service Framework for Older People* (DoH, 2001). These are admirable aims for services for older people. However, most do not impact on the landlord–tenant relationship in the private rented sector, because this relationship is based on the rights and responsibilities of both parties. Privacy seems to be the only value that has close links to the landlord and tenant contract (particularly the covenant of quiet enjoyment).

The situation changes when the landlord is providing an element of care and support: there is then considerable scope for violation of personal boundaries, and values such as autonomy and respect also become relevant.

Table 6: Barriers to reporting elder abuse or harassment

Barriers in reporting elder abuse in general	Applying to older tenants in the private rented sector
The victim may be dependent on the abuser for basic survival and fear retaliation	Yes, tenant is dependent on landlord for shelter, a basic human need
The victim may assume blame for the abuser's behaviour and experience guilt or stigma at having raised a child (or married a spouse) who abuses	Yes, if emotional relationship between tenant and landlord
Fear of being removed from home and institutionalised	Yes
The bonds of affection may be stronger than any desire to leave the situation	Yes, if 'bonds of affection' are with the property because of memories or location (for example, marital home for widow/er)
Concern about jeopardising the family's status within the community	Yes, if ethnic, religious, cultural or family relationship between tenant and landlord
Societal views of the private domain of the family	Yes

Source: Developed by the authors from Penhale (1993)

The elder abuse literature stresses the importance of gender, power relationships and poverty as contributing factors in abuse. It is helpful to bear these in mind when considering landlord–tenant relationships. Landlords and their agents are likely to be male and older tenants are more likely to be female. There is also, by definition, an inequitable balance of power between landlord and tenant. Finally, many older people remain in the private rented sector due to low income and lack of capital.

Overlaps and differences in understanding domestic violence, elder abuse and harassment of tenants in private rented housing

There are useful overlaps and differences between domestic violence and elder abuse (McCreadie, 1996). These overlaps and differences in understanding can be extended to harassment in the private rented sector, as shown in Table 7.

There is criticism in some of the elder abuse literature (in particular, Brammer and Biggs, 1998), about the emphasis on protection rather than legal action. Local vulnerable adult strategies take a problem-solving and mediation approach by the caring professions, and legal remedies are rarely used:

> … elder abuse has been systematically positioned in British social policy so as to focus on domestic settings, but within a welfare, rather than a criminal framework … the relative absence of a tradition of interpreting the lives of older people as subject to abuse … has led to ambiguity concerning the nature of the problem and action that might be taken. (Brammer and Biggs, 1998, p 289)

In housing law the emphasis is on legal action, although agencies (for example, local authority tenancy relations officers) generally approach landlords informally to achieve remedies prior to taking legal action.

The Social Services Inspectorate (1993) recommended that policies on protection should be framed within the context of principles of empowerment. McCreadie (1996) develops this emphasis:

> Empowerment consists of (a) enabling people to know what their choices are and (b) making those choices practicable, feasible choices. The context in which these choices are exercised may involve a balancing of risk with independence. Empowerment of older people might mean more of a focus on domestic violence, or on advocacy, or on more help to the abuser, *or on housing*, or on greater support in the caring role. (p 88; our emphasis)

Table 7: Links between domestic violence, elder abuse and harassment of older tenants

Domestic violence	Elder abuse	Abuse/harassment in private rented housing
Physical and sexual violence, emotional abuse	Also includes financial abuse and neglect	Physical, psychological, financial, sexual, neglect (abuse) Harassment, violence, trespass, intimidation (harassment)
Violence as criminal behaviour	Emphasis on protection	Criminal behaviour or illegal actions under civil law
Violence by men towards women	Violence by men and women towards men and women	Violence and harassment by landlord towards tenant
Violence by partners and ex-partners	Violence by adult children, partners, siblings, friends, neighbours	Violence and harassment by landlord's agents or other tenants toward tenants
Clear victim; clear perpetrator	Ambiguities over victim	Clear victim; clear perpetrator

Source: Developed by the authors from a table in McCreadie (1996, p 18)

Summary

The debates on elder abuse and adult protection have concentrated on abuse in institutional and family care settings. However, there may be scope for using the empowerment approach and multi-agency contacts to assist older tenants, especially if they wish to stay in their existing accommodation. The more there is a relationship beyond the formal legal contract, the more likely it is that such approaches will be essential, because in such circumstances the older tenant is most unlikely to wish to pursue legal remedies for harassment. This issue is developed further in Chapter 8.

5

Experiences of older tenants with their landlords

Introduction

This chapter looks at the conditions experienced in private rented housing by some older tenants, based on fieldwork interviews in the six case study locations in 2001. The focus is given in particular to the relationship between tenants and their landlords. It draws on the 38 tenant interviews, 36 agency staff interviews and the contact with 14 landlords through interviews and the landlord forum. Interviews took place with tenants still in the private rented sector, and with former private tenants now rehoused in social rented housing. Because most were contacted via voluntary and statutory agencies, it is evident that they were more successful in accessing help than those older private tenants who remain isolated and unreached by services. Some minor details have been changed to protect anonymity, and this is also why geographical locations are not stated.

The fieldwork revealed that private tenants experienced different types and degrees of harassment and abuse by their landlords, from verbal and physical abuse to psychological and financial abuse. Neglect, including disrepair of property, was another major form of harassment. Some were one-off incidents, but others were repeat and long-term actions (or inaction). Sometimes landlords were not aware of their action (or inaction) distressing tenants. Indeed, harassment of older tenants can be caused by ignorance of the law. It was evident, however, that in some cases landlords had a clear intention of evicting their tenants through a series of events.

Harassment and unlawful eviction

The following examples indicate that some landlords had a clear intention of evicting their tenants using a combination of direct and implied threats, the use of insults, abuse and occasional bribery. The small but repeated harassment could slowly and skilfully build up fear and distress among older tenants:

> "He harassed me. He wants me out. He rang the hospital to say I'm insane.... My landlord, he came to me and offered me £1,000 to get out, then he said to me, 'Oh! Mrs, you haven't got long to live....' I said where do I go with £1,000?"

An older couple who were regulated tenants suffered from a series of episodes of abuse and harassment after their property had been bought at auction by a new landlord. The landlord sent them a series of abusive letters, and threatened to take them to court for rent arrears, although he was the one who refused to collect rent. The landlord suggested that his relative "would be prepared to swap property with the tenants". The tenants had no intention of moving out of their home where they had been living for their entire married life. A month later, the landlord wrote of his disappointment that the tenants did not want to move, and five days after that sent another letter demanding access to carry out major repairs, including digging up all the floors. The tenants also suffered from a mysterious burglary where, although nothing was taken, a terrible mess was made. A year later, they gave up the tenancy.

Such unreasonable requests are one way of harassing tenants. Some landlords set very unreasonable conditions for rent payment. They may try not collecting the rent to cause tenants to fall into arrears, and thus provide a reason for eviction. They may insist that the rent be paid in cash, sending cheques back to the tenant. One landlord demanded that the rent must be "delivered to my address [a few miles away from the tenants] every Friday by prior telephone arrangements or between 8 and 9.30am any morning or between 5 and 7pm any evening". In another case, a landlady refused to give her bank details to the council so Housing Benefit could be paid directly into her bank account. Consequently, the tenants had to travel across town to deliver the rent fortnightly, until the landlady instructed them to pay her by money order sent by recorded delivery. Both methods incurred extra expense to the tenants.

Disconnecting services can be another means of evicting tenants, which can be intentional or unintentional, as when landlords forget to pay the bills. The research found cases where instead of complaining or reporting to landlords, some tenants continued to live in a house without basic services because they did not want to make any 'fuss'.

While some landlords try to evict their tenants, others try not to let them leave, often from hard-to-let properties. Landlords' refusing to provide a reference or proof of rent is indeed one mode of harassment.

Sources of harassment experienced by private tenants may extend to their fellow tenants. Living in housing in multiple occupancy, in particular, mixing different age groups and thus different life-styles, may cause problems. When young tenants moved in with drug problems or chaotic life-styles, the life of older tenants had become very unpleasant. In some cases, landlords used the tactic of moving younger people into the building as a means of harassing older tenants:

> "I've had 18 months of sheer hell, things stolen off me in the Bed & Breakfast. It was full of young kids, 17, 18, 19, all on drugs. They knew I had a bit of money, and they pinched my food to sell to get a fix."

Another example concerned an older couple in a bedsit in an HMO who had been harassed by younger tenants. A series of events included younger tenants turning off a fridge in the communal kitchen; taking their food (including Christmas turkey) out of the oven while it was cooking; banging on a shared bathroom door when they were using a bathroom; and making a noise late at night.

Financial abuse

A number of types of financial abuse were uncovered during the fieldwork. Owners of rental accommodation operating as Bed & Breakfasts often charge tenants extra money for food. The fieldwork interviews revealed that, in some cases, landlords failed to supply an adequate quantity and quality of food for the charges. One informant complained that the breakfast was very unhealthy because the landlord only provided ingredients for a fried breakfast without any essential items such as milk. In addition, although the landlord hired someone to come and cook breakfast and to clean the house, the person stopped coming due to the landlord's failure to pay for the service.

Over-charging was also reported in running costs for the use of water and meter-operated cookers or electric heaters. In cases of 'inclusive rent', some tenants experienced services being cut off completely when landlords, deliberately or not, failed to pay the bills.

Some landlords tried to charge tenants for their 'hours and services'. On top of setting out unreasonable requests for rent payment, one landlord demanded a "10% charge for expenses and call-out fee to collect rent owed; £20 for the service of returning a cheque; and £2 for writing each letter".

Another type of financial abuse related to the misuse of deposits. Landlords often refuse to pay back rent deposits when private tenants move out. Many landlords often treat rental deposits as their own money instead of money handed over to them in trust.

Other examples of financial abuse included landlords holding the social security books of tenants. Landlords held and cashed the benefit books to cover "extra costs for the bills and services". In one case, a landlord owned a shop attached to a house in multiple occupation where tenants could purchase cigarettes and alcohol on credit. The landlord kept and cashed their benefit books, and the tenants never knew how much they owed or what he had taken. The landlord made them feel constantly in debt.

Amending rent books was another problem: records are important since a rent book is often the only proof of the start of a tenancy, or whether rent has been paid, and may be needed to prove succession to the tenancy, for example, after the death of a spouse.

Privacy and control

Privacy and control was another issue, with three main types of problem uncovered during the fieldwork interviews:

1. *Interference with mail:* landlords open mail addressed to their tenants. One informant called this a 'scanning machine'. In particular, some landlords are interested in the mail sent from the local authority and other benefits offices, which can be identified easily from the envelope.
2. *Calling at the property constantly, without notice, or using pass keys to enter property:* landlords may not think that calling at the property without notice is a mode of harassment. One informant explained that his landlord frequently walked into his room in shared housing to empty a meter. The tenant was often in his room when the landlord walked in "without even knocking". Another complained that his landlord sometimes would stay talking too long. This may be a lack of sensitivity by landlords as much as a lack of legal knowledge, but such action is a breach of the covenant of 'quiet enjoyment' granted to tenants.

    There was a more subtle case of a prospective landlord gaining entry to view a property and its sitting tenants by deception when he was planning to bid for the property at auction. He sent round his wife and a baby first, and visited himself the following day, both without notice. The landlord even started sending threatening letters to the tenants before he became the owner of the property.
3. *Control over the use of property:* some landlords enforce strict guidelines on how tenants may use the property, whether overnight guests are permitted or how many visitors are allowed at any one time. In one particular case, one landlady even told tenants where the furniture should be placed in the house. The tenants were not allowed

to have their tumble dryer inside the house or put up a television aerial. When the tenants wanted to decorate, they had to follow the landlady's instructions about which colours to use in which rooms and they were not permitted to hang any wallpaper.

Repairs and improvement

Landlords not carrying out necessary repairs is a common problem experienced by older tenants in the private rented sector, although landlords may not consider this as harassment of their tenants. Problems can include both emergency repairs, such as fixing a blocked sink, and more general maintenance, including repairing a leaking roof, rectifying inadequate wiring, or installing an adequate heating system in the house:

> "The kitchen was terrible – it was dirty and cold. No one cleaned the kitchen or common areas. Dirty plates piled up in the kitchen." (They were sharing plates, pots and pans)

> "I've been here with different landlords. Things have deteriorated in the premises. And there's never been a lot done, like the stairs are dodgy. He's never replaced anything. The window frames are very, very old, and then we had problems with the rain coming through the roof, and it ran down the walls. We had to get the environmental health officer in to come and have a look at it. And he said straight away, 'This is no condition to live in', and that he [the landlord] had to do the roof. But the ceiling all bowed, and he never did anything to the ceiling, and this has been going on eight, nine, ten years."

The majority of tenants interviewed during the fieldwork felt that a landlord had obligations to carry out repair and maintenance of a property. However, some landlords may feel that the level of rent they charge does not cover the cost of maintenance. In some cases, even with grants provided by the local authority, landlords refused to carry out necessary repairs or improvements:

> "When my husband was alive, three times he painted the windows inside and out but now they're falling to pieces and it's very noisy. I live on

the main road so I asked the council if they would sound proof it, double-glazing. But the landlord wouldn't let them, I mean we didn't ask the landlord for a penny!"

A landlord refused permission for adaptations for a male tenant in his 90s, and wanted to evict him. The council provided the tenant with storage heaters, which did not need the landlord's permission, and he was able to prove that he was a regulated tenant, so the rent was registered. This meant that after intervention by the council, the male tenant had security of tenure, lower rent and the heating he needed.

Others were able to access grants once they knew about them. An older female regulated tenant had heating installed, with the landlord's permission:

"I mean it was cold in the house but now I have the council, they put me in central heating, thanks to [the advice agency], without [the agency staff] I don't think I'd be here."

Some tenants had no problem getting repairs done and no complaint about workmanship. One couple said, "You wouldn't know it wasn't your own, except that if something goes wrong you wouldn't have to put it right". They felt they were better off with their private landlord than in social housing: "We just phone Mr X and he sorts it out straight away. I don't think that would happen with the council!"

The poor condition of a house can cause serious harm to both the physical and mental health of tenants; for example, one older tenant had had gangrene and had to have some toes removed. He sat in a freezing room since the heating only came on at a set time. A link worker bought him an electric foot warmer, which the landlord would not allow him to use. The tenant ended up sitting with his feet in the kitchen oven to keep warm. Disrepair, damp, dirt and over-charging for meters had all resulted in another tenant moving out of shared housing. Living in such a bad accommodation caused him clinical depression and brought on arthritis.

In other cases, it is the tenants themselves who refuse to have repairs and improvements to their rented accommodation. Some tenants felt that the process takes too long and it is thus too stressful or inconvenient. Others opposed the idea of having any change in their living environment even if their accommodation lacks basic amenities such as an inside toilet, or for improvements such as central heating.

An older man in his 70s had lived in his Victorian terraced house since the 1930s. He had inherited the regulated tenancy on the death of his mother in the 1980s. He was single and had always lived in the family home, having cared for his mother in her later years. The WC was still in the backyard and there was one gas fire. The landlord had rewired the house some years before and the tenant had found that those works were quite disruptive at the time. There had never been any discussion about providing an inside WC or central heating, and the tenant did not want the disturbance of any more works. What upset him most was that the external decorations were in a poor state, and that the area generally had gone downhill, with a burned-out house across the street. He was also annoyed that he hadn't had the opportunity to buy the house earlier ('like the Right to Buy for council houses'), and that he had not been informed when the previous owner sold it on.

Potential rent increases after refurbishment were also a major concern for older tenants. One landlord wrote a letter to his tenant with a list of work needing to be carried out, including re-wiring, damp proofing and timber treatment, and digging up the dining room and kitchen floors. The landlord suggested that the tenant then be obliged to redecorate throughout. The landlord also mentioned that once the works were completed he would be able to get at least double the rent that the tenant was currently paying.

In situations where tenants were required to move out temporarily for repairs, an issue was raised as to whether the landlord used the disrepair to evict tenants by relocating them. Under such circumstances, older tenants were naturally reluctant to leave their home, even for a temporary period. One landlord suggested that the tenants may have to move out for a short period of time, at least for three months, due to the work which needed to be carried out being extensive. Although the landlord politely offered to help them with the move and with alternative accommodation, the final words in the letter were taken to be very forceful. There was a clear intention by the landlord to try to evict the tenants.

An older couple lived in a basement flat, which needed substantial repairs. The council served notice, and the couple moved to a flat upstairs during the work. After the works were completed, the landlord would not let the couple move back to the flat. Eventually, the council had to get an injunction against the landlord.

Either temporarily or permanently, the idea of a 'move' often distresses older tenants. If tenants prefer not to move out even temporarily, they may have to put up with disruptions during the work. Some older people also fear being moved into sheltered accommodation or into a care home. Some landlords may exert pressure by saying such things as, "You cannot manage living here".

Change of landlords

Change of landlords can bring distress, or feelings of fear and insecurity, to older tenants. Sometimes tenants have no idea when their landlord changes, since many properties are owned by absentee landlords and managed by letting or managing agencies. With each new landlord, the managing agency can also change; there is thus a constant flux, confusion and worry over who tenants are dealing with. The properties in which many sitting tenants live have been sold off, passed on, or auctioned off several times. New landlords may offer repair and improvement to the property, but this may result in rent increases. Since affordability is a major issue among older tenants, it is again likely to put them under pressure.

> "I came [here] in 1949. The house we're living in we had the upstairs. Now this one's bought it at an auction. He's had it two years. If the council don't pay me any rent [that is, Housing Benefit] I can't send it to the landlord. He sent me two notices to quit. He's a bit of a bleeder. He's put the rent up, and the rent officer's been, and they haven't granted the landlord what he's asked for."

Relationship with 'good' and 'bad' landlords

The research confirmed that good relationships existed between some tenants and their landlords. Some relationships appeared to be based on trust, sometimes without a written contract. Those considered to be 'good landlords' would respond to the needs of tenants promptly and sympathetically, sometimes even beyond their legal responsibility. For example, an older regulated tenant lived downstairs, while assured tenants living upstairs had been effectively acting as carers of the older tenant. When the assured tenants upstairs could not afford to pay the legal rent increase, the landlord reduced their rent so that they could stay and continue to care for the older tenant downstairs.

Although it may sound contradictory, the research also revealed that a good relationship with a 'bad' landlord was possible for some tenants. There were landlords who took in or even targeted disadvantaged people, such as ex-street homeless, prostitutes, and alcohol or drug abusers. Although their rented properties were often in severe disrepair, such landlords certainly provided accommodation for the bottom end of the market. These landlords knew how to maximise their rent income using the benefit system effectively, and often enjoyed a secure rental income from the Housing Benefit available. In one example, a landlord used to bring his tenants down to the local authority office and made sure that tenants applied for their Housing Benefit. Despite several weeks' delay, the benefits were eventually paid directly to the landlord's account. Although this particular landlord used to intimidate both tenants and the staff, it can be queried who else would house such people.

In one example of poor quality shared houses in the fieldwork, there were intimidating notices in the windows stating, 'Polite notice: Anyone caught on these premises if they do not live here will have at least one arm broken and when I'm taken to court the judge can have the same'. The landlord preferred to house all older men, because he felt that they were less trouble than younger tenants:

> "They're OK except they drink a lot when they get their money once a fortnight, but once it's all gone they're OK again. I'm the best unpaid social

worker.... They all refer people to me – housing, social services – but my rents haven't gone up for years. But they pay you [the voluntary agency] £95 per week. Why can't I get that?"

Tenant interviews confirmed that even 'bad landlords' can provide a service. One man, who was disabled, had previously abandoned a housing association property after damage caused by 'friends'; he said that the housing association had told him, "We can take you to court or you can put your notice in". They offered him no advice, so he left and ended up in poor quality private rented housing, with a notorious local landlord:

"Where I am now, it's brilliant, he's a good landlord, he'll do anything for me. I see the landlord now. The flat is as good as, if not better than, the other [housing association] one."

He was scared to say who his landlord was: "He's a very, very private person.... If he knew I'd been talking to you....".

Another, in a shared room, had mixed feelings:

"It's OK, there's worse places to be, like no bed. You get some landlords, they're on your back all the time. I lived in one place [where] you even had a meter for the shower. You've got none of that here, but you've not got your own space. There's not much privacy sharing with someone, but I'm all right where I am for the moment. I've got the keys to the kitchen, some of them are smackheads [drug addicts]. You can't trust them with gas or anything...."

There was certainly a necessity for the services such landlords provided. However, once areas had been gentrified, all the poor quality housing and those landlords who would take anybody were likely to disappear. Tenancy relations officers expressed concern regarding such developments: how would the 'bottom end' of the market be housed in the future?

Furthermore, some complex and problematic relationships were found between tenants and particular types of landlords. In cases where the tenant and landlord are friends, the tenant may not feel able to enforce his rights. Getting necessary

repairs in the house is one example. There was a case of a house in severe disrepair and the tenant had to put a bucket under the holes in the roof when it rained, and also under the drain to the kitchen sink which needed to be emptied every day. The tenant felt obliged to the landlord since the house had been let as a favour.

An abusive case was also found in a mother and son household. An older mother had exercised her right to buy a council house, and then passed it to her co-resident son. The ownership was transferred prior to her death, since she was worried about having to sell her property to pay for the cost of nursing care if necessary. Once status between owner and tenant was reversed, the son had become abusive toward his mother.

Problems may arise when the landlord is an old person, or older than the tenants. The fieldwork revealed one case where an older landlady constantly breached the covenant of 'quiet enjoyment' of tenants. She came around monthly to inspect the premises for the first six months, and also let herself into the property when the tenants were out of the house. Many restrictions were applied to the use of the property and very little autonomy was given to the tenants. The landlady may not have had a deliberate intention of harassing her tenants. As an amateur landlady, her ignorance of the law and what is expected of her, or indeed her strong attachment to the property, may be reasons to explain her unprofessional attitude.

Issues regarding older landlords include tenants becoming at risk of eviction if older landlords die. Beneficiaries may refuse to carry out repairs. They may try to evict tenants in order to move into the property themselves, or realise the asset. For example, one elderly owner-occupier lived on the ground floor and let the first floor to a retired nurse who had looked after the owner on an informal basis for many years. The retired nurse had no security of tenure because she shared the bathroom with the owner. When the owner died, the house was inherited by her relatives. It was in poor repair; for example, the gas fire and hot water geyser were condemned, so the tenant had no heating and hot water. The new owners refused to do repairs as a way of getting the tenant to leave. Ironically, the tenant had a weak case for staying because of having shared facilities with the owner.

When landlords are from the same ethnic background as tenants, they are likely to understand any particular needs. Landlords tend to provide property in the right location, and indeed, living in the right ethnic community can be the most important criterion for tenants from ethnic minority groups. An older Asian man had been living in shared tied housing with other colleagues, above the Asian restaurant where he worked. When his family came over to England, he had to stop working to look after his sick wife. He spoke no English (his interview was conducted with an interpreter). He applied for council housing but the council 'lost' his file. The restaurant owner offered to put him and his wife up in his own family house, where they were still living at the time of the interview. They were overcrowded (10 people in the house) but he knew the area and liked the family, and the rent was reasonable. The relationship with the landlord was said to be good, except that there was pressure because of delays in receiving Housing Benefit.

Overall, the advantages of what landlords offer may sometimes outweigh the disadvantages. Consequently, some tenants have to live in a property that is in severe disrepair or put up with harassment from landlords.

Insecurity and fear of rent increases

Perceived or actual insecurity of tenure was common among the older informants, as was fear of rent increases. It is true that some forms of occupational status do not offer much or any security of tenure (see Chapter 3). Where an assured shorthold tenancy is given, the landlord must obtain a court order before eviction, but it is relatively easy to do this if using the shorthold ground for possession. The second two examples shown above (the retired nurse and the Asian man) are excluded from the 1977 Protection from Eviction Act, which means that no court order is required before evicting the occupant, who has no security of tenure at all.

People who have little or no security of tenure cannot enforce their legal rights or even threaten to enforce their rights without the risk of eviction. This obviously places them at a severe disadvantage in their relationship with their landlord. Fear of eviction can have the same effect, even if it is not a well-founded fear. Some tenants with very secure forms of tenancy, such as a regulated tenancy under the 1977 Rent Act, were fearful of being taken to court by their landlord and losing their homes. People living in insecure tenures, such as licences and assured shorthold tenancies, actually do lose their homes, for example, when they try to enforce their rights to have their homes repaired. The fear of becoming homeless is daunting for many people, but can be particularly so for older people.

A former assured shorthold tenant had moved from her bedsit rented flat in a large mansion block into council sheltered housing, but only with the assistance of an advice agency:

> "I'd like to have stayed there if I could. The trouble was the rent. I was happy – it was convenient, near the station, the shops. I felt safe, but if he gave me a month's notice where would I go? I asked about the council list. They said no, there's lots of people waiting."

Another assured shorthold tenant was still in his tenancy, but felt insecure:

> "My landlord, I've got to know him so well and he's known as a very unpleasant man. But he reckons I'm the best tenant he's got, and every time it comes to throwing me out, I fight and he lets me stay. I'm still there but I think my days are numbered because the council are reluctant to pay the increased rent. The trouble is every time the landlord puts the rent up, he says, 'Well, we've gone to all the estate agents in your area, and we have ascertained that the going rate for your flat is £...'. So the rent officer comes round, and you know he's got to work within certain parameters. If he reckons that the rent your landlord is asking is reasonable, and you can't afford it, you've got nowhere to go. If I can't afford the next time he puts it up, I'm out on the street. I'm on a yearly shorthold tenancy, and if I can't pay he can evict me. This happening every year, it sends you round the bend. He would never have let me have the flat in the first place if he'd known I was DSS, but I managed for the first few months without claiming."

Problems with Housing Benefit occurred for both regulated and shorthold tenants, especially overpayments, as discussed further in Chapter 7.

Ignorance or unskilful use of the law

Interviews conducted during the fieldwork revealed an ignorance of the law among landlords and tenants alike. This is hardly surprising, given the complexity of housing law. However, a lack of knowledge about tenants' rights can lead some landlords to overstep legal boundaries. Marsh et al (2000, p 9) also stated that landlords and housing workers thought that "the most frequent cause of harassment and unlawful eviction [was] landlord ignorance of the law, although some housing workers felt this was used as a convenient excuse". The following are common causes of unlawful action: rent arrears and the Housing Benefit system; delays in possession proceedings; and the changing nature of the tenant population to include more vulnerable households with social problems.

Tenants who do not know about or understand their rights cannot seek to enforce them, and can be more easily coerced into acting against their best interests. Many tenants interviewed did not know what kind of occupational status they had, or the legal rights associated with it. Some tenants assumed that they had more security of tenure than they actually had. One had an assured shorthold tenancy, and believed that the district judge would be able to use his discretion and not grant a possession order. (This is not the case if possession is sought on the shorthold ground; see Chapter 3.) Another man in his 70s thought that he was secure because when he moved in during the early 1990s, the landlord had told him, "That's yours for the rest of your life". He actually had an assured shorthold tenancy.

Tenants and licensees sometimes move out when a notice to quit is received, but they are not generally required to do so. A court order for possession is required before evicting most occupants. Where a discretionary ground for possession is being cited against a tenant, there is a strong possibility that the court will not allow an elderly tenant to be evicted. Although licensees in the private sector have very little security of tenure by comparison, nevertheless the legal process of regaining possession takes a long time to complete. In most cases they will have several weeks before they actually have to leave their home, unless they are 'excluded licensees'.

Regulated tenants under the 1977 Rent Act will normally have a fair rent registered on their property. In order for the landlord to increase the rent, an application must be made to the rent officer, who then sends notification of the new rent being *requested* by the landlord. Reports were received of older tenants simply signing and returning the notification of a landlord's application for a rent increase without question. They were unaware that they could request a consultation with the rent officer, who may in fact award a lower rent increase than that requested.

Some tenants complained that they did not know the name and address of their landlords, and did not know how to contact them. They were unaware of their right to be informed of the identity and address of their landlords. It is a criminal offence not to supply this information when requested to do so in writing (1985 Landlord and Tenant Act, Section 1). If a landlord fails to include his address in a demand for payments of rent or service charges, the tenant can lawfully withhold payment until the information is given (1987 Landlord and Tenant Act, Sections 47-8). Tenants also had problems with managing agents:

> "We don't see the landlord now. Whereas before, when the landlord was here, we had everything done if we ever had anything wrong – sometimes within half an hour. Nowadays it's a case of you go to the agent, and they say, 'Oh yes, we'll send someone'. It could be weeks later when someone comes."

> "Oh Mr X [managing agent] is a very nice man to talk to, but nothing ever happens."

The informants reported a case of elderly tenants being charged a fee of £100 by an estate agency for finding them a property, which is a criminal offence (1953 Accommodation Agencies Act).

Summary

It might be thought that faced with all these problems, nearly all older tenants would have been happy to move out. However, some had no desire to leave what was in some cases their home of many years. One older man had been born in the house he was still living in:

> "Well I like [area] myself. I don't know anybody outside of about a two-mile range. I've got relatives but they live miles away. I never see them – once in a blue moon. I was born here, I'm happy as I am, I want to stay here. I know everyone round here. I don't want to move."

Nevertheless, this chapter has looked at the wide range of examples of harassment and abuse to which older tenants in the private rented sector may be subjected. Chapter 8 will explore in depth how such tenants might be better supported, but first it is necessary to set these individual experiences within a broader housing and social context (Chapter 6), and within the limitations of the present 'system' (Chapter 7).

Living in the private rented sector: the impact of the wider housing market and social and housing policies

Introduction

This chapter develops further the themes first introduced in Chapter 2. Moving on from the historical overview and the current profile of the private rented sector, it examines the importance of the wider housing market and its impact on both tenants' experiences and landlord behaviour. Drawing on the research fieldwork, it examines in more detail the reasons why older people are in the private rented sector, set within the context of wider housing and social policy.

Private landlords and local factors

Although it is commonplace to talk about 'the private rented sector' as if it were an homogeneous whole, the reality is that private rented housing varies enormously. There are two main determinants for such variation: structural factors (the legal and regulatory framework, availability of mortgage finance, taxation policies, alternatives for investment) and local factors (supply and demand of properties, property prices, rent levels). Chapter 2 outlined some of the structural and policy influences on private renting. This chapter explores the importance of more local factors.

The number, size and rent levels of properties in the private rented sector in any area will be affected by:

- the local economy and demand for homes;
- the local housing market;
- the nature of the tenant population in the private rented sector;
- the nature of the stock of residential properties generally available.

The difference that local factors can make is most strongly brought out by comparing two of the case study areas: the northern towns and the London borough. Each case study area has its own distinctive market characteristics which impact on landlords and their older tenants. The contrast is not as simple as between the north and the south. It can also be between inner areas of older housing with a poor environment and outer areas of suburban or rural housing in the same locality. A key feature of the overall housing market in recent decades has been the increasing price polarisation between housing hotspots and declining areas.

In northern town A, much of the private rented housing is small two- or three-bedroom Victorian terraced houses built straight onto the street. In this town, some of these houses could be bought in 2001 (untenanted) for between £10,000 and £18,000. Despite house price inflation across the country in 2001-02, by mid-2002 prices for these small terraced houses had not increased. Many have central heating, modern kitchens and bathrooms and often double-glazing, and are reported to be in reasonable condition. There has been little or no increase in prices since the late-1980s. In fact, in some streets, prices have decreased and houses are now boarded up, with some vandalised, burned out and unsaleable.

Such housing was previously the first step on the housing ladder for young working people. However, regeneration and new housing on brownfield and greenfield sites has knocked the bottom out of the market. Anyone in work, even on modest pay, has been able to get a mortgage and to move into a brand new house on an estate. Such a property has a garden, carparking, domestic appliances, carpets and curtains, and legal fees paid. The developer can offer access to a mortgage (often 100% of the purchase price) and a deposit which can be as low as £100.

This has left the Victorian terraced houses unwanted by new owner-occupiers, so they have remained unsold or been bought up, cheaply, by private landlords. The local housing market had received a recent boost from the arrival of asylum seekers in the town, with the national dispersal scheme's ability to pay higher rent levels (due to the better facilities, furniture and equipment specified).

Rents for such properties range from £30 to £65 per week for single household occupation. The lower rents are for old regulated tenancies, the higher for recent assured shortholds. When let as HMOs or to sharers, rents can be even higher (approximately £30 per room, with living rooms also used let out). Rents have increased very little over the past 10-15 years. There is a plentiful supply of such properties and a shortage of tenants. Landlords will accept people on benefits, and are eager to work with a local organisation running a deposit bond scheme for homeless people to access private renting.

Even 'better' private rented properties can be cheap. One older couple interviewed had an assured shorthold tenancy of a spacious suburban two-bedroom two-living room detached bungalow. Their rent had not increased for nearly a decade: it was £54 per week. The landlord was happy for them to stay, without imposing a rent increase, because they were reliable tenants. They had considered but rejected moving to a housing association sheltered housing scheme, where the rent would have been the same or higher, and the accommodation much smaller.

Northern town B respondents reported the same situation: a surplus of housing, both private and social rented, meant that there was little incentive for landlords to evict older tenants. In both northern towns, older tenants were considered a better bet than younger tenants: more likely to look after the property and do minor works themselves, and less likely to complain. However, in the midlands and the south, older tenants were less popular because, if they had regulated tenancies, the rents were low, and because they were more likely to put down roots. A survey of landlord attitudes in the midlands city found that landlords preferred younger single people, students and childless couples, who would move on quickly, making it easy either to increase rents or to sell the property for the capital gain.

The contrasts between the northern towns and the London borough are particularly striking. The London borough is conveniently placed for commuting to central London. Although much of the borough was traditionally working class, with a considerable amount of private rented property, the areas of 'gentrification' spread during the 1990s, from the more obviously fashionable areas into most parts of the borough. Four older Irish men had been given a cash incentive to leave their rooms in a large period house let as an HMO. The house had recently been sold for over £800,000. Small Victorian houses, similar in size to those in the northern town, were in excess of £300,000 in 2001. Rent levels varied widely, with newer tenants with assured shortholds usually paying the most, but even old regulated tenants had seen large increases in their fair rents at each review. For example, one tenant had their 'fair rent' increased from £30 to £90 per week after the landlord made improvements, and the market rent for a typical one-bedroom flat would be £180 per week. Since the fieldwork conducted in mid-2001, house price inflation has continued to push property prices higher, although rents have stabilised (as at mid-2002).

In northern town A, there were few reports of landlords trying to get tenants out. They could not profit from evicting tenants since the properties were worth so little. There was evidence of harassment and abuse at the worst end of the private rented sector, but it was not linked to property prices. Landlords did not expect capital gain; they feared capital depreciation. They were in the private rented sector primarily for income from rents. For these reasons they had no incentive to do more than the minimum repairs, and had no incentive at all to make improvements to the property.

In the London borough, there was plenty of evidence of landlords wanting to profit from price increases. Potential landlords were reported to seek out older people with regulated tenancies, sometimes even calling at their properties. Older tenants complained that properties frequently changed hands without their knowledge. Landlords often wanted to make improvements but older tenants were suspicious of their motives and in many cases did not want the disruption. A number of tenants reported attempts to get them to leave. These ranged from incentive payments and suggestions that they would be better off in sheltered housing or a care home to threats and harassment such as the 'builders from hell'. Similar factors were apparent in all the case study areas. Older tenants were frequently in competition with other prospective tenants who were likely to be more profitable for the landlord. In the south coast town, a voluntary sector housing advice agency, quoted in a local newspaper, said:

> "Right now it's a landlord's market. There's a huge demand for rented property and price rises have given landlords the chance to cash in, either by charging very high rents or selling properties at a huge profit. Landlords are being tempted to sell up and move on, leaving tenants in the lurch."

Private tenants in the context of wider social and housing policies

Life course factors

Although the focus of this study is older people, it is absolutely crucial to understand that, for many, their difficulties stem from past policies towards certain groups of younger people, particularly those on low incomes who were either single or childless. Their disadvantaged position in the labour market and society, as well as housing policies, has often resulted in them ending up in a less privileged housing tenure.

For single women in particular, who had neither equal pay nor a male breadwinner in their household, their disadvantaged position in the labour market could be another contributing factor for being unable to establish financial stability, and thus they experience poorer housing situations in later life.

Until the 1970s it was difficult for a single woman to obtain a mortgage, and she would not have been considered a priority for council or other social housing.

The same life course factor can be applicable to male migrant workers in the post-war period. The research fieldwork revealed that there are a number of male migrants who came to Britain alone, remained single, and whose housing career has been less successful compared with their married counterparts. As migrant people in the days of 'waiting lists', they were ineligible because they did not meet residency qualifications. If they moved from place to place following jobs in the construction industry, there was no chance of building up enough 'residency' anywhere. Then, when 'housing need' replaced simple queuing, they were ineligible because they were single and without dependants. In one case identified in the fieldwork, one man had succeeded in being allocated council housing, but he was still penalised. Since he became homeless, he did not have a choice about where to live and was placed in a 'rough' area. After enduring cold (the whole flat was heated by a single electric fire), break-ins, climbing 12 flights of stairs when the lifts broke down, and loneliness, he returned to the private rented sector.

For this group of men, housing has not usually been considered a priority on which to spend money. One man, when asked if he had ever considered buying as an option, said that he preferred drinking if he had money, so he then had no spare money for a house. Another man explained how he saw the intertwining of life course and housing situations. He had witnessed a situation where the landlord had a shop and allowed drink and cigarettes on credit, and said of the other tenants:

> "These guys were institutionalised into social-rot [by the landlord and the system created by him]. People are so used to it [alcohol] and cannot leave."

He added that a broken marriage or relationship breakdown sometimes leads them into a situation where the easy access to alcohol exacerbates the problem.

Among all the older households in Britain, single elderly households are over-represented in the private rented sector, see Table 3 in Chapter 2. Single older people are much less likely to own their homes, and much more likely to rent from a social landlord, both local authority and housing association, compared to older couples and other multi-person households headed by an older person (Leather, 1999).

Evidently, marital status is one of the major factors which determine people's access to home ownership, and thus their housing situation in later life. High percentages of older residents who live in privately rented accommodation also appear to have no family.

The research fieldwork also came across older people who had remained in the private rented sector because of their caring role. There are variations on a number of themes here. Some stayed in the rented homes of their family members (parents, uncles, aunts) as carers and then inherited the regulated tenancy. This is another important factor in causing some older people to remain in the private rented sector: unmarried adult children (especially women) were traditionally expected to remain at home as carers for their elderly relatives. This affected their ability to have paid work and access other forms of housing. One woman had given up her flat in the south east to move north, nearer to her widowed father. This story is complicated, however, because the father had bought her the flat in the south east and told her to stay put. Moreover, after she had moved to be nearer to him, he moved away. There is a suggestion that the need was as much the daughter's as the father's, something which may be another factor to understand in considering the housing needs of single people.

The other route into rented housing for carers is for those who have been paid carers, whose accommodation has been linked to their job. The Elderly Accommodation Counsel database, for instance, showed regular enquiries about rehousing options received from people who were wardens in

sheltered housing or housekeepers in private households and who, on retirement, needed to find a new home. Some have retired, remaining in the home of the person cared-for, but with an unclear tenancy or employment status. Others continue in a caring role into their old age, and then become homeless when the person they have been caring for dies or needs to go into residential or nursing care. These are the sorts of situations where there is often a close, quasi-family relationship between carer and cared-for person, which complicates the traditional landlord–tenant role. Members of the extended family of the person cared-for may be sympathetic, but they are more often interested in the capital value of the house than the needs of the carer.

Single people have also tended to be disadvantaged when accessing affordable social housing on a long-term or permanent basis, given the housing allocation policies of local authorities. In the pre-war period, when private renting was the major form of tenure and the number of social housing units was small, such allocation policies were relatively unimportant (Malpass and Murie, 1999). With the growth of council housing in the first half of post-war period, 'having large families' was originally defined as one of the priority preferences which local authorities had to consider when allocating their council housing under the 1957 Housing Act.

Moreover, in the last two decades, when council housing stock has become increasingly scarce due to the Right to Buy, the decline in new construction, demolition and stock transfer, a priority for housing allocation has remained focused firmly on the family. However, some single tenants in the study had experienced living in council housing in the past, having often been allocated accommodation as a one-off deal (following clearance, for example). The fact that approximately a third of single elderly households are currently council tenants (Table 8) may therefore be explained by the fact that they have

Table 8: Tenure by single households headed by a person aged 60 or more in England 1995 (%)

	Own outright	Buying on mortgage	Council tenant	Housing association tenant	Private tenant
Single male	43	6	35	7	9
Single female	48	4	33	6	7

Source: ONS (1996)

been widowed or have been allocated a property as an older person rather than as a single person in the past.

Furthermore, home ownership has become the most popular type of tenure among British households in general, but the meaning of home ownership can be different for families and for single people. Compared with rental accommodation, home ownership can bring many advantages, such as the provision of security and stability (reducing the fear or threat of being evicted), social status, and the accumulation of assets in the form of housing. Indeed, home ownership can be used as a means of accumulating wealth, which can be passed on to the next generation within the family. In this context, single people without children may not have a strong incentive to purchase or maintain their own home, and choose to remain in the rented sector. To illustrate this point, one female informant described the advantages for her of renting privately:

> "I want security and peace of mind with no need to worry about maintenance. Also, I am not married, so I have no children to leave a property."

Needs that the private rented sector meets

Older tenants being 'left in the lurch' when a landlord sells up illustrates an important though different point: that the needs of older people are sometimes better met in the private rented sector than in social housing.

In addition to life course factors from their earlier life, people who have previously lived settled lives as owner-occupiers or social housing tenants may want, or need, to move in later life for a variety of reasons:

- being nearer to relatives (especially with adult children being more mobile because of the job market than in the past);
- following marital or other relationship breakdown, when there are insufficient funds to buy separate properties for owner-occupiers, or the social housing tenancy stays with one party and the other has to leave;

- following financial problems such as business failure or repossession;
- on returning from time spent living abroad.

At the time that accommodation is needed (often at short notice), the waiting list for applicants or transfers for social rented housing can be a barrier, or there may be no appropriate or acceptable social housing available in the area required. Older people are competing with single people of all ages for 'general needs' social housing, including people with specific needs and disabilities. Because of the over-supply of sheltered housing in most areas of the country, older people are likely to be steered in that direction, whether or not it is their preferred choice. Some housing providers have policies of only offering bedsits to single older people, reserving one-bed flats for couples. Consequently, older people in such circumstances often turn to the private rented sector when they need accommodation, or because of the lack of alternatives they remain in private rented housing even if there are problems with housing conditions or landlords.

Some of the tenants in the case studies remained in the marital home because of emotional attachments, or because of its size or location compared with alternatives on offer in social rented housing. Others found private rented housing quicker and easier to access than council or housing association properties, especially if they wanted to move nearer to relatives or had to seek alternative housing following relationship breakdown. The price differential has been reduced as public sector rents have risen: in some areas, private rented housing is no dearer, and it can be in a better location or condition than some of the public sector housing on offer.

However, respondents also expressed concern about the difficulties for older people who had accessed the private rented sector while still working (especially assured shorthold tenants in the south where market rents were high), but who could no longer afford the rent once they retired and were extremely anxious about their future, knowing that the rents would continue to increase.

In all of the case study areas the private rented sector also plays an important part in providing accommodation for people with a history of homelessness, drug/alcohol abuse and/or mental health problems. Many of these people (especially single men) end up in HMOs, usually in bed-sitting rooms with shared facilities. Both this study and other research (Hawes, 1997; Crane, 1999; Pannell et al, 2002) have found that there are a number of issues arising from this.

Older people who have led an unsettled way of life have been used to accessing forms of accommodation which are now no longer available to them. People working in mobile jobs, such as the construction industry, used to move around the country, staying with landladies, in common lodging houses or other dormitory-style hostels and very poor quality hotels. Single men leaving jobs with 'tied' accommodation, such as the hotel and catering industry, or the Armed Forces, often ended up in these types of accommodation as well. For those who could not access hostels, there were night shelters as a last resort. During the 1970s and 1980s, however, dormitory-style accommodation was considered unacceptable in the modern world and much of it was closed down.

Today, the common lodging houses have all closed, and most of the landladies appear to have disappeared. Organisations like the Salvation Army have upgraded their dormitory-style hostels and replaced them with modern hostels with single rooms, but fewer beds. There has been a corresponding increase in small-scale, better quality, shared supported housing, but most of this is not direct access and it is nearly all aimed at young people. Hostels and night shelters are also dominated by younger people. It is reported that many of them are drug-users, and there is often a clash of culture between older and younger residents.

The rise in homelessness among young people and the government's desire to end rough sleeping have changed the emphasis of such services: they now want to work with users in the short term, encouraging them to address their problems, to move on and to meet targets from their funders. Older people either want to remain in the hostel and make it their long-term home, or are reluctant even to go there in the first place. They are not prepared to enter the 'professionalised' voluntary sector and to undergo the risk assessment, the needs assessment, the

key worker interventions, the life-skills training and so on.

As seen in Chapter 5, many of these older people (particularly older drinkers or those with mental health issues, personality disorder or challenging behaviour) therefore end up in the 'bottom end' of the private rented sector, where no questions are asked and there is no attempt to get them to change their behaviour. Of those who want to stay on in what is now re-designated as a short-stay direct access hostel, there is concern from the professionals that the direct access provision is silted up with older long-stay residents. From the older people's point of view, they want something more like the old-style 'caring landlady', or even the dormitory-style hostel, with food and laundry supplied and other people to talk to. Some of these older people end up leaving the hostel and going to the private rented sector, in shared houses or HMOs. They do not want to live in what other people consider better quality council or housing association housing, such as a one-bedroom flat on their own: they do not see quality in terms of physical standards and tenancy rights, and they would rather have personal contact with an unfriendly landlord/landlady than none at all.

Lack of diversity in social housing provision for older people is a form of ageism. Research funded by the London and Quadrant Housing Trust (Brenton et al, 2002) has looked at the problem of ageism in housing policy and its implications for the social rented sector. One conclusion the team has reached is that lack of diversity comes about because there has been an assumption that all older people may be treated as an homogenous group, and that provision may therefore be standardised. With a few honourable exceptions, local authorities and housing associations alike have been content to provide housing units for older people that are all very similar. Centralised financial constraints from both government and The Housing Corporation make it very difficult for any social landlord to do anything different. In our case study areas there were housing officers and voluntary groups who could see the need for different kinds of provision, tailored to the needs of different older people. In some places, they were optimistic about making some progress, but in general the first issue is to recognise the general lack of real choice, and the second is to think of new ways of providing it.

The private rented sector can be used to create new housing schemes of good quality similar to some found in the public sector. As part of their empty property strategy, one case study local authority has been working with a private landlord to convert old industrial sites into residences for older people. The local authority provided some of the capital (£3 million) from their Single Regeneration Budget, and the landlord raised the rest of the capital from private sources. The council gave the money on condition that the landlord accepted tenants from their waiting list, and that the rent officer fixed the rents (£60-80 per week). The local authority officers reported that there is a real sense of community among the residents and no security of tenure problems. There is a housing manager living on the site, who looks after the tenants if they have problems. The landlord developed the scheme because he had altruistic motives, although he does make a profit out it.

Summary

The position of older private tenants in the six case studies needs to be understood in the context of the nation's housing stock and housing policies as a whole, and in the context of the particular local housing market. The complex interaction of supply and demand, economic prosperity, Housing Benefit rules, tax rules, the financing of new social housing and the regulation of tenancies and housing standards all affect the well-being of older people in the private rented sector.

At an individual level, life course factors and policies in public and private sectors alike pushed certain groups into the private rented sector when they were younger so that they now constitute this group of older tenants. Single men and women on low incomes, itinerant workers of all kinds, childless couples on low incomes: these are some of the groups who were not able to buy and who did not qualify or were not a priority for council housing, thereby also missing out on the 'Right to Buy'.

Government policy since 1988 has been to make renting more attractive to private landlords, and most landlords appear to prefer tenants who are not going to stay too long. If the Law Commission's proposals to reform the law relating to occupational status and security of tenure are enacted, the status quo will be

continued. The Law Commission's view of current rented housing provision is that social housing is there to provide for the long-term housing needs of those people who are particularly vulnerable within the housing market, while the private sector caters mainly for people who are not seeking housing on a long-term basis. Its Consultation Paper states:

> [Private] Landlords are, in the main, providing accommodation to niche sectors of the market who in general fall outside the scope of social housing and many of whose tenants are not seeking to be housed on a long-term basis. The private sector now exists within a market framework. Although the potential for exploitation of tenants by landlords remains, changes in the housing market mean that, these days, there is less need for the State to guarantee long-term security of tenure. Rather the relationship between the landlord and the occupier can be mediated by the terms of the contract, a contract which under ordinary principles of consumer law must be fair, and in relation to which breaches may be remedies in the same way as other breaches of consumer contracts. Nothing in this paper will prevent private landlords from enhancing their contracts with occupiers by including a greater degree of contractual security of tenure than the minimum required by the legal framework we propose. (2002, para 1.23)

This is bad news for older tenants who want a permanent home. The research has revealed how little access older tenants have to the legal processes that are meant to protect them (discussed more fully in Chapter 7). Interviews disclosed that there may indeed be some private landlords who would want to offer good security of tenure, but they appear to be in a small minority. The ageing group of regulated tenants are increasingly vulnerable to illegal pressure to leave, while assured shorthold tenants face the joint insecurities of rent increases and possible eviction. The message from the government would seem to be that it is not policy to use the private rented sector to provide permanent homes for older people, but does not answer: what is to be offered instead?

Lack of choice and lack of varied provision for older people in the social rented sector is another factor that now keeps some older people with their private landlords. Those who want more space or less space, those who want minimal rent and maximum spending power, those who don't want to leave an area they know and in which they are known: these are the people whose needs have to be understood and met in appropriate and more diverse and imaginative ways.

7

Problems with 'the system': making life more difficult for older people in private rented housing

This chapter considers the problems and tensions caused to older people not by their landlords, nor by other tenants, but by external factors: the systems and public organisations with whom they must interact.

Some older people consider that such issues are a form of elder abuse. Action on Elder Abuse found that a small percentage of calls (3.7%) to its helpline were about what it termed 'societal abuse'. This falls outside Action on Elder Abuse's definition of elder abuse, describing cases where callers felt that statutory services were not responding to their needs (Jenkins, et al, 2000). As discussed in Chapter 5, the research disclosed that many older informants had the same feelings.

The research found that the Housing Benefit system was one of the major sources of tension between older tenants on low income and their landlord. The other major problem area was the difficulty of accessing and enforcing legal remedies.

Housing Benefit administration

Local authorities have a variety of roles and responsibilities relating to older people in the private rented sector, including:

- administering Housing Benefit and Council Tax Benefit;
- tenancy relations;
- housing and environmental health services;
- housing advice services;

- rehousing services (including referral to other social landlords);
- enforcing public health law on housing conditions;
- administering grants for repairs, improvements and disabled facilities;
- facilitating multi-agency work, and working with private and social landlords;
- area renewal policies.

This chapter focuses on Housing Benefit because it is the main problem area. Chapter 8 discusses the role of other local authority services.

There have been a number of reports expressing concern about Housing Benefit over recent years, and a large number of ombudsman cases (Age Concern London, 2001; Audit Commission, 2001, 2002; Kemp et al, 2002). The Housing Policy Green Paper (DETR, 2000b) acknowledged that the Housing Benefit system has serious deficiencies, and in April 2002 the government introduced Housing Benefit/Council Tax Benefit performance standards for local authorities in England. These cover seven functional areas, including customer services and the need for speedy and accurate claims processing. The Audit Commission point out that this is the first time that performance standards have been set for benefit administration, and that they "now make clear the importance of obtaining information as quickly and efficiently as possible ... [which] increases the ability to get it right from the start" (Coxon, 2002, p 29).

This research confirms their findings: Housing Benefit is a problem for tenants of all ages in all tenures, but older private tenants suffer most because of both their age and their fear of arrears and eviction. Being in rent arrears is shameful to a generation brought up not to get into debt, and it causes enormous worry, anxiety and real damage to physical and mental health. It also puts tenants at actual risk of eviction, particularly those tenants with assured shorthold tenancies.

Application and renewal procedures

People in the current older cohort are often reluctant to apply for welfare benefits. Some expressed their strong feeling towards independence – "I have managed my life without benefits up to now, and can carry on". Various other reasons can be considered to explain why some older tenants do not approach the local authority for advice and assistance, which may include their ignorance of available services and their unwillingness to upset the landlord.

However, the application procedure and documentary evidence required for assessment also make the system inaccessible for some older tenants. Filling in a complex and lengthy application form is certainly an obstacle for some older tenants, especially for those who have poor literacy skills. Producing a much-simplified version of the form would help older people stop rent arrears where they sometimes failed to re-apply within the time limit because they could not read or tackle such a complex and lengthy form.

The need to re-apply for Housing Benefit each year is a particular problem, especially as this is not the case for other means-tested benefits, which run on from year to year. This point was also made by the Audit Commission and the government has recently announced that from mid-2003, pensioners will be awarded Housing Benefit/Council Tax Benefit for a period of five years.

Some local authorities had introduced a simpler renewal form, but anti-fraud measures stopped such common-sense approaches. If someone forgets to re-apply, or the form goes astray, it is very difficult to get the claim backdated, even with the involvement of advice agencies. This is at least partly because local authorities used to get backdated benefit reimbursed from central government, but some years ago, limits were imposed, so much of the cost of backdating now falls on the local authority.

Measures introduced by central government to prevent fraud were widely considered to have made the situation worse. Now, the verification framework requires that benefits administration sees 'original documents'. There is also a requirement for a visit to ascertain that a new claimant is actually living at the address. One landlord complained that when the Housing Benefit officer visited his older tenant who was an alcoholic, his benefit was stopped. The decision was made since he was not 'in residence' because he spent most of his time on a park bench with his acquaintances.

According to agency staff in one case study, there was no guidance on how to interpret such regulations, although officers did have to justify their decision of stopping the benefit if they were challenged. The problem is that vulnerable older people do not often know how to challenge. People who move from room to room in a shared house may also experience similar problems. For example, it was explained how an older man moved to a room next door in the same house, and his move was picked up when he renewed his Housing Benefit claim as the form asks where your room is located in the house (for example, back, front). Since the rent was identical, there was no fraud in this case. He lost six months' Housing Benefit and had to pay it back, even though he was on a low income. He was reported to have appealed, but lost on appeal. Even advice agencies cannot always help in such a situation.

Confidentiality rules

Landlords and agency staff have problems due to confidentiality rules. Applicants may choose whether to have the benefit paid directly to the landlord (many prefer this method) or to receive it themselves. Under the former system, landlords cannot tell if their tenants have complied with the regulations and made prompt application for Housing Benefit: all they know is that rent stops coming in. Confidentiality rules prevent the Housing Benefit section from giving landlords any information about why benefit has stopped. Advice agency staff are not necessarily kept informed either, even when the benefit officers are aware of the involvement of agency staff in the case. An example of this was an Asian older women who was shocked to receive a telephone call at home one Sunday about a complex problem with her claim, even though an adviser had been involved for some months. The tenant was instructed to go to the benefits office at 9am on the Monday morning. Both the tenant and the adviser felt that this was a deliberate ploy to prevent the tenant consulting the adviser first.

Delays caused by processing claims

Severe delay in Housing Benefit payment causes a major problem in tenant–landlord relationships. Despite the national regulation that all new claims should be assessed within 28 days from the date of application, in some areas applicants have waited up to 12 months. As a result of delay, some tenants may receive threatening letters from their landlord. It also causes concern to tenants:

> "For a long time, five or six months, they [Housing Benefit office] did not pay any rent to my landlord. I went to see my councillor. She could not understand why it took so long because there was no change in my circumstances.... Because he [landlord] is not getting his rent, even if I have a problem, I hesitate to tell him. I've paid for things myself like mending the storage heater. I've spent over £200 of my own money ... I'm worried the landlord will get fed up and evict me."

Benefits staff were reported to use administrative devices to help meet their targets and to get round the time limits, which only start to run once all the relevant information is received. The verification framework is a major reason for delays, while applicants submit all the necessary documents. Photocopies are no longer accepted: benefits staff have to see originals. Documents may be lost in the process, causing distress to older tenants and delays to claims being paid.

Many landlords now require deposits and rents in advance, thus cutting out Housing Benefit claimants, especially in areas with booming housing markets. Landlords who are prepared to house benefit claimants experience serious difficulties with the system. Such delay in payment is problematic in itself, but there is also no guarantee that the tenant's application will be successful.

Furthermore, there are a series of problems caused to older (and indeed younger) tenants because Housing Benefit does not always cover the full rent. As a

means-tested benefit, the tenant's income may be too high for 100% entitlement. This can be a particular problem for older people who have some savings, and/or a small occupational pension, but there are three other reasons, all of which will leave the tenant paying a top-up out of their limited incomes, namely unrealistic reference rents, service charges, and under-occupation.

Unrealistic reference rents

There was widespread concern about the relationship between the Rent Service and Housing Benefit within each local authority. The Rent Service is an executive agency of the Office of the Deputy Prime Minister. The Rent Service has two main roles: setting 'fair rents' for regulated tenancies, which can be reviewed every two years, and setting 'reference rents' for Housing Benefit for assured and assured shorthold tenants, and also for people with no tenancy, just a licence.

Until 1996, a private sector rent could only be restricted for the calculation of Housing Benefit if it was above the market level for that particular dwelling, if the accommodation was deemed to be too large, or if it was considered exceptionally expensive for the claimant to occupy. In 1996, concern about exploding Housing Benefit expenditure resulted in the introduction of two additional restrictions: the local reference rent, for tenants of all ages, and the single room restriction which only applies to young single people under the age of 25. The local reference rent is the average market rent for dwellings of a particular size in the locality, and becomes the ceiling for the rent on which Housing Benefit is calculated.

Agencies and landlords in most case study areas reported that the statutory procedure used in assessing 'reference rents' for Housing Benefit limits produces unrealistic rent levels. Despite the original intention, 'reference rents' set by the rent officers often do not reflect true market rents. A broad locality is chosen, and they knock out the highest and lowest rents and then take an average of the rest. Since 'reference rents' are often lower than market rents, tenants usually end up paying a top-up out of their limited income. In 1999, 70% of cases referred to the rent officer had their benefit assessed on less than the full rent (Kemp et al, 2002). This is problematic, particularly in areas with rising rent levels, such as the south coast town and the London borough. In one case study, where the Housing Benefit system was administered relatively efficiently by the local authority, an officer explained her frustration in relation to the Rent Service since she did not feel that 'reference rents' reflected true market rents or were realistic:

> "Rent officers rarely visit properties, so how do they know about the market values? That is why when they do visit, the agreed payment is almost always increased."

Rent officers seemed consistently to undervalue properties. Their response was that people should look for somewhere reasonable. When the Housing Benefit officer was asked what she wished the most at the end of the interview, her reply was to "get rid of the rent officers" since they "are totally unrealistic" and look at much too wide an area to obtain the 'reference rents'.

Local authorities have very limited discretion to pay Housing Benefit above the reference rent level and it is usually cash-limited. In one case study area, the local authority had an annual allocation for discretionary payments of just under £200,000. In two months in 2001, they had over 130 applications. If such an application is successful, it is a continuing commitment from year to year.

The system takes no account of the condition of the property when assessing the reference rent. It militates against landlords letting better quality properties, since they get the same rent from a poor quality property as they would from a well-maintained counterpart, if they fix their rents at the levels of reference rent. Both landlords and agency staff complained that there was no incentive for 'good landlords'.

Service charges

Housing Benefit does not cover food or non-eligible services such as heating or hot water, which are sometimes included in the rent (usually in Bed & Breakfast or bedsit accommodation). The Department for Work and Pensions (formerly the Department of Social Security) sets national rates for non-eligible items such as food and heating, but these have remained the same for many years. Some landlords over-charge their tenants for services. It is not unusual for landlords to charge between £10 and £15 a week on top of rents to cover heating and hot water for shared housing.

However, some tenants actually preferred this arrangement of 'inclusive rents', despite the fact that they were often over-charged. It is advantageous for those tenants who lack the life skills needed to manage their everyday life, by removing the responsibility of handling bills.

Under-occupation

Another problem with Housing Benefit is the effect of regulations concerning under-occupation. If someone is considered to have more rooms than they need, their Housing Benefit will be limited to the reference rent for the number of rooms that they are considered to need. This rule creates a problem in areas such as the northern case study where small two-bedroom terraced houses are the predominant types of property available for rent, and there are hardly any one-bedroom flats. A single person or even a couple can be considered to be over-housed, so their rent is not covered in full. Yet for many older people, the idea of having to share housing is unlikely to be acceptable. The system is not flexible enough to allow discretion because of the local housing market.

This rule applies both in the private rented sector and housing associations, although it may be less rigorously enforced for housing associations. It applies to the number of rooms rather than other measures of space such as floor space. Thus it encourages landlords of HMOs to maximise income by further sub-dividing large rooms to cram more people in, or even, in extreme cases, of having two to four people in a room. For example, a notorious local landlord in one case study area had several small two- and three-bedroom houses, housing two to four people per room (8 to 12 people per house). The tenants ranged in age from 17 to 70, male and female were all mixed in the same house and sharing all facilities. The tenants paid £40 per week each to the landlord, £30 from Housing Benefit, and £10 top-up not covered by Housing Benefit. His properties were estimated to produce a gross income of £16,000 to £25,000 a year, per property, 75% paid through

Housing Benefit, but the rest through other incomes of the tenants to cover the service costs.

Reclaiming over payments

Tenants, advice staff, landlords and their managing agents all reported problems with rules on reclaiming overpayments of Housing Benefit, which also linked to the lack of information they received from benefits administration. The entitlement to benefit lies with the tenant, but tenants often like their benefit paid direct to the landlord, and landlords prefer this, some insisting on it. However, if a landlord receives direct payment, s/he has to undertake to repay any over payment.

Over payments (alleged and actual) can arise for a number of reasons, the most common being changes in circumstances such as the tenant receiving an extra or increased income. They can also arise because of mistakes by the benefits staff: the fieldwork revealed some serious and unacceptable 'mistakes', including such fundamental errors such as counting Disability Living Allowance/Attendance Allowance as income when it should be disregarded for calculating entitlement to means-tested benefits. Some over payments are caused by actual fraud, although with older people it seems likely that most are caused by failure to understand the complexities of the benefits system, or simply forgetting to declare something.

Advisers reported dreadful cases of tenants receiving numerous incomprehensible computer-generated letters demanding repayments, sometimes going back years, due to misunderstandings or oversights: this caused great anxiety. It seems likely that hearing such tales on the 'grapevine' is a key factor in dissuading older people from claiming means-tested benefits such as Housing Benefit and Income Support. Such problems arise more frequently with older people due to the likelihood that they will have a combination of income and savings, including small occupational pensions and small amounts of savings spread across different savings accounts.

Problems arise when the benefits administration demands repayment of an over payment, perhaps many months or years later. For the tenant, they do not have the money to repay; for the landlord, it will probably result in a loss, as they are unlikely to be able to recover it from the tenant, who may even have left

by then. This is another reason why 'good' landlords are reluctant to take people on benefits unless they are letting in an area where there is no one else. No doubt landlords would also argue that it is a reason for charging higher rents to people on benefits if they are able to, to compensate them for such problems.

Housing Benefit: the way forward?

Overall, the shortcomings of the Housing Benefit scheme make landlords less willing to let out their properties for people in receipt of Housing Benefit, particularly in areas of high demand for student accommodation and from employed people with cash. Chapter 8 includes specific recommendations to improve the benefits system for older private tenants and refers to recent government announcements concerning Housing Benefit reform.

Lack of age-specific records

None of the local authorities in the case study areas kept comprehensive records or monitored the ages of tenants who contacted them. Housing and environmental health departments dealing with the private sector or performing tenancy relations roles often appear not to have recorded the ages of the caller or of the person who was the subject of the call, if it was made on behalf of someone else. Some records were kept relating to disability and ethnicity, and names and titles helped identify the gender of callers, but the lack of details kept about the ages of callers prevented the research team from collecting robust quantitative data specific to elderly private tenants.

Omitting to record ages of callers meant that none of the local authorities could monitor trends in age-related problems. This hindered the formulation of policies and procedures to deal with problems that are common among older tenants (or among any other age-specific group, for that matter), or to plan for anticipated needs of older tenants. Some key informants speculated that the numbers of older tenants in the private rented sector were quite low in their locality. All of them stated that older tenants tended not to contact them or to complain. This may or may not be true, but it may also mean that there are hidden problems among this group. Local policy makers may not have a good understanding of the make-up of the tenant population and thus cannot consult with them in a meaningful way. Enforcement officers cannot track trends or plan preventative action: as one local authority respondent said: "We haven't got figures that would enable us to have a more considered approach".

The police do not keep records of 'age' under the 1997 Protection from Harassment Act, although 'race' of callers is recorded. Therefore they also cannot monitor trends in age-related problems.

Mullins et al (1997) noted that there was a long-standing recognition that recording systems in housing advice services are weak, and that they are often developed with families in mind, rather than older people. Parry and Means (1999) also found weaknesses in the collection of data about enquirers to advice services; they recommended that basic information, such as age, ethnicity and disability, should be routinely collected by all agencies providing housing advice. Otherwise, whether the service is reaching particular groups cannot be measured.

Barriers to access to justice

Chapter 5 highlighted that some of the factors that prevent older private tenants from obtaining legal redress are due to personal circumstances. Others are problems within the legal and social support systems.

In Chapter 3 the rights of private sector tenants and licensees were set out, and the legal remedies available to victims of harassment, poor management, disrepair and illegal eviction were outlined. The remedies for harassment and illegal eviction were considerably strengthened by the 1988 Housing Act, and tenants' rights to have their properties kept in repair are also quite good, at least in theory. But how effective are they in practice? What sort of protection can they offer victims of ill-treatment?

In this section the experiences of agencies and individuals that have tried to pursue legal remedies will be discussed. There are a number of barriers that prevent good access to justice for victims of abuse and harassment, which are considered below.

Lack of knowledge about advice services

Many older people are quite isolated and cannot or will not take advantage of support services. People living in such circumstances often do not know what advice services exist, or whom to turn to if they have a housing problem or a problem with their landlord. Advice agencies often do not advertise their services, because they are already working at maximum capacity and are unable to deal with any increase in demand (Genn, 1999). Consequently, unless tenants are in contact with other support services, they may not get referred or know about where to go for legal advice.

Fear of or lack of confidence to use legal proceedings

Tenants' advisers reported that older people are generally reluctant to take legal proceedings themselves, and some tenants were disillusioned by the failure of council officials or the police to take action on their behalf. Being involved in court proceedings is stressful, and tenants often felt that the law would favour their landlords in any event. Fear of legal costs was a deterrent to some tenants, who were consequently reluctant to consult a solicitor. Courts can be intimidating places for those who are bringing proceedings and for witnesses, and some older people were fearful of being involved in court proceedings. The fear of experiencing further victimisation is a genuine and well-founded fear for some people. While these fears are common for many people regardless of their age, for those who are frail and elderly they can present insurmountable barriers to seeking or using legal remedies.

Non-eligibility for publicly funded legal help

Eligibility for Community Legal Services (CLS) funding (what used to be called 'legal aid') depends on the income and capital of the applicant. Older people are often disqualified from receiving funding because of their savings. They are also often reluctant to dip into their savings for essential items, and even less inclined to spend them on legal fees. At the time interviews were conducted, the capital limit for legal help was £1,000, which excluded many pensioners, even though they had very low incomes. On 3 December 2001, the capital limits for legal help and help at court went up to £3,000. The gross income cap has been raised to £24,000 per annum. Even if the applicant is financially eligible for public funding, before it can be awarded the CLS must decide that the possible outcome warrants the expense of the proceedings, which can present problems in some cases.

As stated above, a number of older informants reported that the fear of incurring legal costs deters some people from seeking legal advice from solicitors. Voluntary advice agencies do not charge for their services, but there may be other difficulties in accessing their services.

Time limits for legal proceedings and other procedural problems

Local authority officers reported that they experienced procedural difficulties in prosecuting landlords for illegal eviction and harassment. Some offences, such as those under the 1997 Protection from Harassment Act, are summary offences, and prosecutions are begun by the issue of a summons rather than by indictment. The time limit for starting proceedings after the commission of a summary offence is six months, and the difficulties in collecting evidence means that cases sometimes cannot be brought within the time limit. The burden of proof in criminal proceedings is that the offence must be proved 'beyond reasonable doubt', which is a very high standard. A lot of evidence must be collected and corroboration obtained where possible, but local authorities are limited in their powers of investigation. Under the 1977 Protection from Eviction Act, Section 7, for example, they have the power to request in writing that a managing agent reveals the name and address of a landlord, but that takes time. They do not have the power to require other agencies, such as utilities companies, to give them information that they may need to provide corroboration of harassment. One tenancy relations team had identified the need for more training and had recently been on courses about interviewing techniques and giving evidence in court.

Even when proceedings are begun, there may be other bureaucratic or procedural delays that inhibit successful prosecutions. One local authority reported that they consider about 40-50 cases of harassment or illegal eviction per year are suitable for prosecution,

yet they are only able to bring 10-20 cases per year (these figures are for private tenants of all ages, not just older tenants). Tenants are reluctant to go through the process, which takes one to two years. Cases are hard to prove, and it is sometimes difficult to get evidence. The victims move on in their lives and change addresses. Since the evidence of the occupant is crucial, prosecutions would have to be dropped in such cases.

Attitude of the courts

Informants reported that even when prosecutions are brought, the courts tended not to treat landlord harassment very seriously and imposed relatively low fines. Marsh et al (2000) found a similar concern with the level of compensation awarded by the courts in civil proceedings. This meant that in some cases it was more profitable for a landlord to illegally evict someone and take the consequences than it was to follow the legal procedures. For the victim, watching the landlord get off fairly lightly can cause disillusionment with the legal system.

Summary

There are major problems with the Housing Benefit regime, which bear particularly harshly on older people. Although this is also true of housing association and council tenants, older people in the private rented sector are even more disadvantaged. Council and housing association tenants are more likely to have access to advice and support to deal with benefits problems than isolated private sector tenants, and they are less likely to be evicted.

There are also problems both with accessing the legal system, and with specific aspects of the enforcement of tenancy rights. Our research points to the singular failure of the legal system to protect older tenants from unlawful actions by landlords. Chapter 5 gave some extreme examples of the kinds of misbehaviour and harassment perpetrated by people who are either calculating or uncaring in their actions. Marsh et al (2000) have recommended changes in the law of harassment to address some loopholes and to make the law more effective. Discussions with older tenants and with agencies that support older tenants suggest, however, that using legal proceedings to address their problems is rarely going to be an option for older tenants. The barriers are too great, particularly the stress and the fear of the loss of their home.

The conclusion reached from the data collected in the fieldwork was that for older private tenants, it often made no difference whether the tenants knew their rights and sought advice, or meekly departed as soon as the landlord asked them to: determined landlords would win in the end by wearing down their older tenants.

8

Supporting older people in private rented housing

Introduction

In many cases problems are experienced by private sector tenants generally, but the vulnerability of many older people makes them less able to deal with their difficulties and more in need of support than others in similar situations. This chapter explores how best to support older people in the private rented sector, whether they wish to stay or move out. It acknowledges their reluctance to seek advice and support, describes examples of good practice found during the research, and comments on other changes which could make life better for older private tenants.

The role of advice services

Parry and Means (1999) highlighted the need for improved communication and collaboration between the range of specialist and generalist agencies (both statutory and voluntary) working with older people. It is clear that local authorities and other agencies need to be proactive in publicising their services to older private tenants and to older people more generally.

In this research, both staff and older people identified that one of the main roles of voluntary sector organisations was to act as information provider, advocate and broker between older tenants and the relevant statutory service, reassuring older people that their views and preferences would not be overridden. For example, advice staff in one case study area stressed how important it was to get older people to feel 'comfortable' about seeking advice; they felt that

calling it 'legal' advice was off-putting to older people.

Parry and Means (1999) found that, with a change in emphasis, advice services can reach disadvantaged groups and a range of older people. They carried out an evaluation of five different projects funded by the Housing Associations Charitable Trust to develop housing advice for older people. They concluded that:

> By targeting and promoting specialist services, the needs of older people for information, advice and advocacy can be met effectively. This applies across a range of different agencies that currently provide advice and support services. What is needed is an understanding of the needs and wishes of older people and a service that is provided where older people go. (p 26)

It should be noted that the agencies studied by Parry and Means had received funding specifically to provide advice and support for older people. This presupposes the recognition of the need for such advice services for this group of people and the willingness and commitment to try to meet that need. On a more positive note, the government has begun to stress the pivotal role of advice services within its multi-agency homelessness strategy (DTLR, 2002).

Tenancy relations, environmental health and home improvement grants

The role of environmental health officers (EHOs) and tenancy relations officers (TROs) is crucial for older private tenants. All local authorities have EHOs, although they have a wide remit, so the priority given to housing will vary between authorities. Their responsibilities for private rented housing concern the condition and facilities of buildings. Not all authorities have specialist TROs with responsibilities for those aspects of the landlord–tenant relationship which do not concern the building, such as illegal eviction. TROs are generally only found in larger authorities; elsewhere their role will be undertaken by housing advice staff.

Some local authorities have a specialist 'private tenancy team' with housing officers and EHOs working alongside each other, while in others staff remain in two sections or departments, but still cooperate on specific issues. There is one authority in the case studies which established a 'brand name' and is carrying out training for partner agencies, including Citizens' Advisory Bureaux, the police and their area housing offices.

This authority had been through Investors in People and identified the need for further training, which had improved their performance in dealing with landlords. Their training had included a course in investigative interviewing from the Civil Service College, a course on giving evidence in court which included cross-examination with a barrister, and the Police and Criminal Evidence (PACE) training which included using tape-recorders and interpreters. They have since found that taping interviews with landlords and their solicitors has been an extremely effective technique.

Negotiating with landlords, rather than using their statutory powers, is a valuable means to solve problems, as a staff member from another local authority stated:

> "Landlords are encouraged to get in touch with us for advice. We have a duty to both landlord and tenant. Some landlords adopt a belligerent attitude, and a lot of them are ignorant of the law.

> They think it's their house and they can do what they like with it. We always try to approach landlords in a reasonable and constructive way. We don't want to start off on the wrong foot, but they know we'd be down on them like a ton of bricks if they did anything blatant. They know we are going to prosecute if necessary."

This authority was proud of its Chartermark and had clear policies and procedures, which were enforced. However, staff from other local authorities admitted that notices were too often served but not enforced, especially where there had been high staff turnover.

The joint Department for the Environment, Transport and the Regions and Department of Health publication *Quality and choice for older people's housing: A strategic framework* (DETR, 2001a) refers specifically to the particular difficulties of older people living in poor housing, the need to shift the emphasis "to protecting people rather than preserving properties", the important role of home improvement grants, especially for central heating and home security measures. Most of the emphasis is on owner-occupiers and there is no specific mention of older people living in the private rented sector, although there is general comment about the importance of advice agencies.

This research confirmed the importance of home improvement grants and the London borough was particularly active in making grants for improvements in private rented properties such as central heating and new windows. Most unfitness is now lack of amenities, particularly heating (for example, only one coal fire or portable electric heaters which are expensive to run and potentially hazardous). Lack of heating, perhaps combined with ill-fitting, draughty and insecure doors and windows, is a particular problem for older people, as exemplified by the excess of winter deaths in the UK caused by fuel poverty.

The advantage of grants like the Home Efficiency Energy Scheme (HEES) is that there is no rent increase for improvements carried out at the tenant's instigation with a grant (although there is if the landlord pays). The London borough also used its in-house Home Improvement Agency (HIA) to facilitate works in some cases. However, some landlords refused permission, as they are allowed to do; there is no enforceable right for the tenant or the local authority to enable improvement works to take place in the face of such refusal. Another problem is that grants and access to the HIA service are more restricted than in the past: in this authority, the applicant has to be actually in receipt of means-tested benefits (not just eligible for them), so people who are too proud to claim, or just over the capital or income limits, miss out. Grants are also usually cash-limited so may be more freely available in some areas than in others.

In a London borough, the local Age Concern had a handyperson scheme, and this too was available to private tenants. Voluntary agencies with handyperson schemes or HIA services (such as Care and Repair organisations) also provide such schemes, but mainly for owner-occupiers. The difficulty in obtaining consent from their landlord often prevents private tenants from receiving such services.

Relationship with landlords: partnership or regulation?

There has been discussion for many years about the merits of licensing arrangements for both private landlords and managing agents. The government has been consulting on changes in this area, especially concerning HMOs, for which there have been manifesto commitments since 1997. Managing agents often have more contact with tenants than landlords (especially absentee landlords), so their role can be as important; research found that 37% of all tenancies involved a managing agent (Crook et al, 1995).

Most discussion around licensing and registration has centred on HMOs, since many HMOs have been badly managed, overcrowded, unfit and in serious disrepair, as discussed in Chapter 2. At the time of writing this report (mid-2002) proposals had been made in legislation before Parliament to strengthen the regulation of HMOs. However, the progress of the Bill had been hampered by parliamentary manoeuvrings, and it was thought unlikely to become law (*Inside Housing*, 17 May 2002).

There has been more general consideration over recent years about the question of regulating the private rented sector, not just HMOs. This question is crucial for this research, since the evidence suggests that although many single older men are in HMOs, there are also many older people in both regulated and shorthold tenancies. A focus only on the regulation of HMOs ignores the needs of these other older tenants.

In their recent report *Chains or challenges?*, Rugg and Rhodes (2001) reflect the diversity of views about regulation, from Shelter's desire for regulation across the whole sector (Shelter, 1999) to the Association of Residential Letting Agents' backing for self-regulation (ARLA, 1997). They conclude:

> ... it seems unlikely that consideration will be given to regulating the sector in its entirety.... The Government ... envisages no role for universal, over-arching measures.... The preference is for improvements in the sector to be achieved by strengthening and revising existing legislation, and creating the conditions in which market and industry-led improvements may be fostered. (pp 20, 22)

An alternative proposal is to stress partnership. The current trend is for local authorities to seek to establish voluntary accreditation schemes and local landlord forums. These policies can produce good results by improving communication between the private sector and the local authorities and by affording a means of educating landlords about their legal responsibilities. These schemes were evaluated by the Centre for Urban and Regional Studies, University of Birmingham (DETR, 2001b). Their findings indicated that due to the voluntary nature of such schemes, only 'good' landlords are likely to join such schemes, and it is harder to recruit landlords in areas of high housing demands. This means that the local authority is geared up to concentrate their enforcement work on 'non-registered' and 'bad' landlords. Almost all of the schemes investigated targeted properties rather than landlords, so landlords could choose which of their properties to enter into the scheme. In a few areas, however, landlords were required to submit all of their properties for approval, which amounted to accrediting the landlord instead of the property.

A number of the case study local authorities had set up forums for private landlords. Like the proposed voluntary accreditation schemes, the problem is that only 'good' landlords tend to attend such forums. For example, in the London borough, between 30 to 90 attend an annual forum out of their database of 1,300 landlords, while in one of the northern towns 50 to 60 were said to attend regular forums, although only 11 were there at the forum which was observed.

It would seem that a new consensus is developing around the potential role that the private rented sector can play, even though there remain disagreements about how best this can be achieved. In 2001 Shelter established the Private Rented Sector Commission, with support from the Joseph Rowntree Foundation, and with a wide range of members: private landlords, tenants, local authorities, academics, housing providers and the voluntary sector. The subsequent report of the Commission focuses on investment, management and regulation (Shelter, 2002). It calls for a statutory expectation that landlords should be 'fit and proper', and for remedies for sub-standard management, alongside greater investment in local accreditation schemes and the voluntary codes promoted by landlord organisations.

Supporting People: towards a wider choice of housing and support options?

Older tenants may need additional support, either in their existing private rented housing or by moving elsewhere to receive support. The case studies found examples of both these options. One of the problems to date has been that older people have generally needed to move house in order to access support (for example moving into sheltered housing to access warden services). Such services were not normally available to private tenants who wanted to stay in their existing accommodation.

Another problem has been that private landlords providing support services paid for through Housing Benefit were subject to no quality controls or regulation for the support services provided, although the property itself is probably subject to regulation (for example for HMOs). Examples include older people living in HMOs where the rent has included a charge for low-level 'counselling and support'. The

research found some examples of this, especially for older men from minority communities. The other significant group is older people with particular needs (usually mental health or learning disabilities) living in HMO-type provision with intensive (and often high-cost) support provided by the landlord/landlady. Such provision is often similar in style to a registered care home, but is outside the care standards regulatory framework if the help is classified as support rather than personal care.

In order to address both these and other issues, from April 2003 a major change to funding of support services will come on stream. Supporting People (DTLR, 2001b) will take over the funding for support services to people of all ages and with a wide range of needs (such as women escaping domestic violence, people with learning disabilities or mental health problems, drug users, ex-offenders). For older people, it will fund the cost of services including supported provided by wardens in sheltered housing, mobile or community wardens, community alarm systems and visiting or residential support staff. Previously these costs have have been met by Housing Benefit for people on incomes low enough to qualify (DTLR, 2001b). The Supporting People Grant will be administered through local authorities in partnership with housing and support service providers.

The expectation is that Supporting People will enable a wider choice of both housing and support. In principle it should make it easier for an older private tenant to receive services from a choice of providers in their existing housing, not just from their current landlord. It should also mean that people do not have to move into sheltered or supported housing in order to access support, but can access services (such as a community alarm system and/or mobile warden) in their existing accommodation, at no cost if they are on a low income.

The introduction of Supporting People will also affect private landlords of HMOs and similar provision who have, until now, been claiming Housing Benefit for services classified as support. Although this is a small section of the private rented market, it is especially likely to contain vulnerable older people. A number of agencies in different fieldwork localities expressed concerns that some landlords (especially those providing lower-level support) were likely to withdraw their service and sell up or change their client group rather than go through the process of claiming through Supporting People. This would then lead to a loss of provision for particular client groups (especially from some minority communities).

Two other issues have caused concern to homelessness and advice agencies. The first is the requirement for an assessment of the tenant's need for support services in order to access Supporting People funding in the future. The second is that, in order to be paid for support costs through Supporting People, there has to be a contract between the local authority and the support provider/landlord. These are significant changes from the previous system. When Housing Benefit covered support charges, there was no needs assessment, the tenant claimed the benefit and the landlord's role was limited to confirming the level of rent and support charge. Some advice and homelessness agencies have expressed concern that, with the new system, vulnerable older people may be unhappy with their private landlord having a much greater knowledge and involvement in personal details about their health and income.

Changes to Housing Benefit

Following all the recent reports and concern expressed about Housing Benefit, as discussed in Chapter 7, moves are now under way to remedy the problems. However, there are difficulties in reforming anything as complex as Housing Benefit, a point acknowledged by the Audit Commission (2002). Discussing the report, a senior manager from the Commission is frank:

> The [HB funding] regime is complex and lacks transparency.... Reducing complexity is no easy matter, since many suggestions fail to balance the conflicting priorities of speed of payment, the cost of the scheme (£10 billion in 1999/2000), and guarding against fraud ... ultimately the trade-off between costs to the public purse and easier access for the claimant is a political one. (Clackett, 2002)

In addition to the performance standards now introduced, the Department for Work and Pensions has recently announced major changes to Housing

Benefit to be piloted in 10 pathfinder local authorities. These include standardised fixed-rate amounts of benefit to provide 'shopping incentives' for private tenants to look for lower rents in what the housing press described as "the biggest shake-up of Housing Benefit since it was created (*Inside Housing*, 2002).

The problem with the new proposals for older private tenants links with the concerns expressed in Chapter 7 about reference rents and under-occupation. The new fixed-rate housing allowances based on family size and location will be calculated using local reference rents, so single older people are likely to continue to be disadvantaged. The proposals have received a mixed reaction, with a pathfinder council commenting: "We are concerned that certainly people do not suffer as a result. We would need to be confident that any standardised Housing Benefit did not leave people out of pocket." Two landlord associations pointed out that rules allowing councils to claw back over payments and the fact that they pay in arrears remain major deterrents. A London local authority reflected: "There's good evidence that people at the bottom end of the market have no choice. The idea of shopping incentives is just not the real world."

For older private tenants, there are a number of specific actions linked to Housing Benefit administration, which would make their situation easier, some of which already take place in some localities, or in relation to other benefits. It seems extraordinary that a benefit which is paid for nationally out of general taxation should be subject to such enormous variety of implementation procedures between different localities.

The first action, which is so obvious as to be hardly worth stating, is that benefits should be calculated within the target time-scale and that administrative devices should not be used to circumvent this. Yet this seems to be beyond the ability of some local authorities, despite numerous reports and ombudsman cases.

More specific remedies include: improving the application and renewal procedure, such as introducing home visits to older claimants for completing forms and abolishing the need to re-apply every year for people aged over 60/65; better liaison between statutory agencies and with voluntary agencies; and changes to Housing Benefit and rent setting regulations.

As discussed in Chapter 7, there is a need to improve the system of the Rent Service so that 'reference rents' are more realistic. The problem appears to lie partly in the practice of taking too broad an area, and not visiting enough properties, and partly in the implied desire to cut back Housing Benefit expenditure. There would be staffing and cost implications for the Rent Service to carry out more visits, and to the Housing Benefit system in meeting higher rents.

The public availability of the Rent Register is known to cause problems to older regulated tenants; it would be safer for them if the document were not public, but it is unlikely that this would be acceptable to government. An alternative would be for rents to be published for an area without giving the exact addresses. The form for re-registration applications should be redesigned to make clear to older tenants that they should not sign it if they object to the rent, and that they have the right to a consultation. A national leaflet stating sources of advice would also help here.

Vulnerable adults policies: the role of social services

As discussed in Chapter 4, local authority social services departments are now required to develop multi-agency policies to prevent or remedy exploitation and abuse of 'vulnerable adults', including older people, as set out by the Department of Health guidance in *No secrets* (DoH, 2000a). The definition of a 'vulnerable adult' is taken from the work of the Law Commission (1993 and 1995) and the Lord Chancellor's Department (1997): a person "who is or may be in need of community care services by reason of mental or other disability, age or illness and who is or may be unable to take care of himself or herself, or unable to protect himself or herself against significant harm or exploitation" (DoH, 2000a, pp 8-9).

No secrets recognises the same five types of abuse as Action on Elder Abuse: physical, sexual,

psychological, financial or material abuse, and neglect, but also recognises discriminatory abuse as an added category. Possible perpetrators include professionals, volunteers, other service users, relatives, carers, neighbours, strangers and people who target vulnerable people. In the context of the private rented sector, this research came across examples of what could be construed as harassment or abuse from:

- professionals: landlords or their agents; benefits staff;
- relatives/carers: landlords/landladies where there was a kinship, friendship or carer element in the landlord–tenant relationship;
- neighbours, especially other tenants in shared housing such as HMOs;
- people 'who target vulnerable people', that is, landlords who set out to exploit vulnerable older people.

No secrets recognises that 'vulnerable adults' (of any age) may both understand and accept certain risks, and prefer to remain in their accommodation despite the risk, and that they have this right to self-determination. However, it is recommended that it is often important for a vulnerable adult to be away from the influence of the abusive person in order to be able to make a free choice about how to proceed.

The right to self-determination is important to bear in mind when considering options for older private tenants. This research found a number of older people who appeared to prefer staying with their private landlord even though their living conditions were poor and they were at risk of abuse and harassment.

There is also a particular problem for older tenants who are subject to abuse from their landlord or other tenants, in that they are unlikely to be willing to leave their accommodation to escape the 'sphere of influence' of the landlord, due to the risk that they will then lose their accommodation. Indeed, there is a potential conflict here with the normal practice of TROs and housing advisers: they would sometimes advise someone suffering harassment not to leave, even temporarily, because it is then much more difficult to get back into the property.

There was plenty of evidence that older tenants will resist leaving for building works, even temporarily, because of their overwhelming fear that they will never be able to return home. Housing advice agencies found that they had a dual role in such cases: supporting people to stay when that was their choice, or brokering the search for alternative housing which was acceptable to the older tenant in cases where they were willing to leave. The multi-agency aspect of adult protection strategies could be helpful here, in that housing departments are supposed to be involved in the formulation and implementation of local adult protection measures.

Summary

This chapter has explored a number of options for improving the support of older people. The role of advice services, environmental health/home improvement interventions and new forms of partnership with landlords were all profiled in terms of their potential contribution. The chapter went on to consider the need for both a wider choice of housing and support options together with a major overhaul of the Housing Benefit system. The chapter concluded by emphasising the potential role of social services authorities through their lead role in the development of vulnerable adult policies.

9

Recommendations

This chapter presents some positive suggestions for improvement of the situations and problems identified in this research. Since a detailed analysis of each issue was presented in Chapters 6, 7 and 8, this chapter is limited to the presentation of the main (selected) recommendations.

Re-introducing a secure form of private sector tenancy

Chapter 6 highlighted how the security of tenure regimes that presently exist under the 1977 Rent Act (which deals with regulated tenancies) and the 1988 Housing Act (which deals with assured and assured shorthold tenancies) can place regulated tenants in a very vulnerable position. The 1977 Rent Act gave regulated tenants very good security of tenure, which most private sector tenants under the 1988 Housing Act do not have. Since January 1989 most tenants in the private sector have been given assured shorthold tenancies, which have very little security of tenure after the first six months. The 1988 Housing Act also removed rent control, and substituted market rents. With regulated tenancies, landlords can only apply for increased rents every two years under the fair rent regime. The 1988 Housing Act permits more frequent rent increases, and at market levels. The problem caused by the two-tier system is accentuated by the recent boom in the housing market, where landlords can expect higher rent profit if rents truly reflect the market rates, as well as higher profits by selling their property for the capital gain. It can also place regulated tenants in a vulnerable position if their landlords are unscrupulous.

Interviews with older tenants also highlighted the detrimental effect that the threat of eviction can have on older tenants' well-being, whether it is a real or imagined threat. So strong is the need to stay in their current accommodation for some older tenants that it acts as a positive deterrence to challenging or standing up to their landlords in any way, even if their living conditions are poor. Clearly there is a need to ensure that private sector tenants can obtain tenancies with good security of tenure if they want and need it. This would require a major shift in government policy, as the Law Commission's proposed changes in the law (Law Commission, 2002; see Chapter 3) merely reproduce the status quo in terms of private sector security of tenure. The proposals fail to recognise the need of many private sector tenants, and older tenants in particular, to have a home where they can stay without fear of eviction, provided they comply with the terms of their tenancy agreement. The Commission's Consultation Paper states (2002, para 1.23) that there is nothing to prevent private landlords from offering the more secure form of tenancy, referred to as a 'Type 1 tenancy'. However, given the attraction of shorthold tenancies for private landlords, some incentive would have to be created for them to offer a Type 1 tenancy to their tenants. There is a need to encourage a different, more professional, landlord who may, for example, receive tax benefits in return for offering rented housing on a long-term basis.

Recommendations

- Changes in the law should be made to re-introduce a secure form of private sector tenancy alongside assured shorthold tenancies, and incentives should be given to encourage reputable and responsible private landlords to offer tenancies with good security of tenure.

Regulating the private rented sector

As discussed in Chapter 2, many HMOs have been badly managed and are overcrowded, unfit and in serious disrepair, and the private sector generally is less well maintained than the social rented sector. In recent years there has been some consideration about the need to regulate the private rented sector, including both private landlords and managing agents (see Chapter 8). The current trend is for local authorities to seek to establish voluntary accreditation schemes and local landlord forums. These policies can have good results by improving communication between the private sector and local authorities and by affording a means of educating landlords about their legal responsibilities and encouraging them to maintain their properties to a good standard. However, due to the voluntary nature of the schemes, only 'good' landlords are likely to join, and it is harder to recruit landlords in areas of high housing demand. Almost all of the schemes investigated targeted properties rather than landlords, so landlords could choose which of their properties to enter into the schemes. In a few areas, however, landlords were required to submit all of their properties for approval, which amounted to accrediting the landlord instead of the property.

The government is endeavouring to introduce tighter regulation of HMOs and has consulted on the creation of mandatory licensing of private sector landlords in areas of low housing demand (DTLR, 2001c). The research for this project, however, revealed that poor management of private rented sector housing is not necessarily limited to areas of low housing demand. Four of the six case study areas experienced high demand for private rented housing and, nevertheless, provided examples of very poor management. Given older tenants' extreme reluctance to enforce their legal rights and the barriers they experience in trying to obtain good quality advice about housing problems, there appears to be a need for a licensing system that applies across the private rented sector generally. Consideration

also needs to be given to increasing the penalties for unlawful behaviour by landlords.

Recommendation

- Private landlords and managing agents should be required to belong to an accreditation scheme, regardless of the types of properties they let.

Amending law and regulation in relation to older tenants

Various issues concerning law and regulation in relation to older tenants were raised in Chapters 5, 7 and 8. Local authority officers interviewed reported that they experienced procedural difficulties in prosecuting landlords for illegal eviction and harassment. The time limit for starting proceedings after the commission of a summary offence (such as the 1997 Protection from Harassment Act) is currently six months, yet the difficulties in collecting evidence mean that it is very difficult to bring a case under the 1997 Act within this time limit. The problem with meeting time limits was sometimes compounded when the victims were older tenants, because of their reticence in making complaints or seeking advice. The burden of proof in criminal proceedings is that the offence must be proved 'beyond reasonable doubt', which is a very high standard. Even when proceedings are begun, there may be other bureaucratic or procedural delays that inhibit successful prosecutions.

There may be human rights implications in any suggestions to extend time limits or relax the burden of proof for criminal prosecutions. Yet the criminal law and procedure as it stands makes the criminal justice system an ineffective tool for the protection of older tenants, who generally do not want the stress involved in trying to get someone to bring a prosecution on their behalf.

Civil proceedings have the same drawbacks as criminal proceedings in terms of the stress involved, and there is a further barrier in the lack of availability of public funding. As discussed in Chapter 7, older people are often disqualified from receiving CLS funding due to their (sometimes even meagre) savings. The capital limit for legal help is currently

£3,000. The research found that the fear of incurring legal costs deters some people from seeking legal advice from solicitors. Those who do want to take proceedings against their landlord may have difficulty in finding a solicitor or law centre with housing law expertise.

Given the difficulties in overcoming these obstacles, local authorities need to be proactive in preventing harassment and eviction. A starting point for improving information and assistance to older tenants would be the imposition of a duty on local authorities to have a tenancy relations service. They already have a duty under the 1996 Housing Act to provide free advice and information about homelessness and the prevention of homelessness. The 2002 Homelessness Act requires local authorities to publish a homelessness strategy at regular intervals. Clearly, having officers whose responsibility it is to advise and, where appropriate, to intervene in cases of harassment and illegal eviction would encourage a more proactive response from local authorities and assist in the prevention of homelessness.

Recommendations

- Local authorities should have a statutory duty to provide a tenancy relations service.
- The government should consider re-categorising the offences under the 1997 Protection from Harrassment Act as being triable either way. This would remove the six-month time limit for bringing prosecutions, and would give investigating officers more time to prepare their cases.
- The capital limit for legal help needs to be increased to at least the level used for eligibility for other public funds such as personal care services.

Reforming the Housing Benefit system so that it better meets the needs of older tenants

The Housing Benefit system is another major source of tension between older tenants on low incomes and their landlords (see Chapter 7, which presented the detailed analysis of the scheme). Severe delay in payment of Housing Benefit is one example, and

another notable issue is the gap between an actual rent and a 'reference rent' which tenants are expected to top up out of their limited income. The need to re-apply for Housing Benefit each year is also problematic, although that point has now been conceded with effect from mid-2003.

There are a number of specific recommendations linked to Housing Benefit administration, some of which already take place in some localities, or in relation to other benefits. These will make a significant contribution to the welfare of many older private rented tenants.

Recommendations:

Better application and renewal procedure

- developing and implementing a simplified, user-friendly application form for older people;
- home visits and telephone completion of claims made by older people, including partnerships with voluntary agencies to facilitate take-up.

Better liaison between statutory agencies and with voluntary agencies

- having a nominated older persons' liaison officer at the Housing Benefit office and the local Pensions Service office, who can be contacted by advice agencies;
- a marker on the computer system for older people to trigger action if Housing Benefit is not reclaimed (instead of just lapsing the claim);
- links between Housing Benefit administration and TROs and EHOs to facilitate referrals;
- a national leaflet to be sent out by the Rent Service with rent registration documents informing regulated tenants that they should consider claiming Housing Benefit if they are concerned about a rent increase, and also consider seeking advice, together with a list of advice agencies available locally and nationally.

Changes to Housing Benefit and rent setting regulations

- reform of the 'reference rent' system, and the rules on under-occupation and on repaying overpayments;
- allowing advice/older people's agencies or council offices to verify documents and pass on to Housing Benefit administration;

- some discretion to benefits administration, and guidance stating that a presumption of innocence must be used, especially for backdating and in cases where there is no fraud or even change in benefit payable

More training and education for the police and service providers

Chapter 3 outlined available legal remedies for harassment and illegal eviction by articulating who actually has the power to prosecute offences under different Acts. For example, local authorities have considerable powers to control poor housing conditions under the 1985 Housing Act and the 1990 Environmental Protection Act. But the research identified that service providers need further training to improve their performance in dealing with landlords (see Chapter 8). Moreover, in terms of offending behaviours by landlords, only the police can bring a prosecution under the 1997 Protection from Harassment Act, but police officers are often under the impression that it is a civil matter, not a criminal offence.

Recommendations

- More and better training for local authority housing and advice workers, magistrates and County Court judges is required to improve the process of bringing harassing landlords to justice and to impose penalties that reflect the seriousness of the offending behaviour. The Police and Criminal Evidence Act (PACE) training undertaken by housing officers in one authority is a useful example. Also, further education among police officers is needed to correct the misconception of harassment by landlords being a civil matter.

Keeping age-related records

As discussed in Chapter 7, in contrast with characteristics such as ethnicity and disability, none of the local authorities in the case study areas kept comprehensive records or monitored the ages of tenants who contacted them. Housing and environmental health departments dealing with the

private sector or performing tenancy relations roles often appear not to have recorded the age of the caller or of the person who was the subject of the call. The police do not keep records of age under the 1997 Protection from Harassment Act, although race of caller is recorded. Omitting to record the age of callers meant that none of the organisations could monitor trends in age-related problems. This hindered the formulation of policies and procedures to deal with problems that are common among older tenants or to plan for anticipated needs of older tenants.

Recommendation

- In order to inform policies and strategies for meeting the needs of older people, it is strongly recommended that relevant organisations, including local authorities, the police and voluntary agencies, routinely collect basic information on age along with ethnicity and disability.

Providing more funding for support and advice services; and creating specialised advice services for older people

There is an insufficient number of organisations that have the expertise to offer help and advice to older private tenants suffering landlord abuse or harassment. TROs exist in only some authorities, partly because the local authorities have only a power and not a duty to act. Even authorities who do have staff may not have enough to meet need. Elsewhere, private tenants may be referred to the authority's general legal services, where it is likely there will not be sufficient specialised knowledge. Changes to the funding of legal aid have led to the majority of legal aid solicitors in private practice withdrawing from the service or not taking on any new clients. The Legal Aid Practitioners group says that young people entering the legal profession are deterred by lack of adequate funding from entering publicly funded legal services. The £3,000 capital limit would also disbar many tenants. Law centres would be able to help in such cases, by funding the work from sources other than that of the Legal Services Commission, but there are only 48 law centres in the whole of England, with an additional one in Wales and one in Northern Ireland. They, too, are under great pressure.

Citizens' Advice Bureaux, much valued as being widely known, independent and non-stigmatising, are also under a burden of great demand, for increasingly complex information, and have little security of funding. To back up the various short-term, charitable sources, they need secure, committed local authority funding.

Recommendations

- There should be a general policy of increasing (perhaps doubling) resources for advice, including grants to law centres and Citizens' Advice Bureaux and of making such funding more secure. In particular, committed core funding from local authorities is needed. Some Citizens' Advice Bureaux have specialist housing services, but even where they do not, all the Bureaux have access to second-tier back-up specialist advice from the National Homeless Advice Service, which is a partnership between Shelter and the National Association of Citizens' Advice Bureaux. Extra resources for these general advice and legal centres is an important way to ensure that there will be a safety net of accessible advice necessary for a problem that may be too uncommon in some areas to warrant a specialised service, or, where there are TROs, as a route through which older tenants may be directed to them.
- The recommendation in the Department for the Environment, Transport and the Regions' report on *Harassment and unlawful eviction of private rented sector tenants and park home residents* that: "local authorities should be required to have either a tenancy relations officer or a clearly identified officer with tenancy relations activities in their job description" (Marsh et al, 2000, para 6.69) should be implemented, and combined with advice to local authorities on their duties to investigate. It would ensure that there were expert officers to whom any cases picked up could be swiftly referred.

Supporting and planning alternative housing solutions

Chapter 6 highlighted that the failure of social housing to provide for a diversity of people with different needs and backgrounds, with a diversity of locations and housing types, is another factor that keeps some older people in the private rented sector. For economic and political reasons, most council housing has been built in estates, and those who do not fit in with the cultural hegemony of the estate will not be comfortable living there. Housing associations who bought up existing housing were more likely to have a variety to offer, but scattered properties are hard to manage and old properties are expensive to maintain. The tendency has therefore been away from such purchases towards newly built properties in small estates. Not everyone has their needs well met by a social rented sector that, under pressure from government, increasingly provides a standardised, uniform product.

People who have previously lived settled lives as owner-occupiers or social housing tenants may want, or need, to move in later life for various reasons. Also, older people sometimes give up homes they own or leave tenancies where they have good security of tenure only to find they have made a serious mistake. The Elderly Accommodation Counsel database provides many examples, such as people moving abroad, people moving in with relatives, and people trying residential care. Once the mistake is realised, these people could then find no housing other than the highly insecure private rented sector.

Recommendations

- Specific support in the form of directives and funding should be given to council housing authorities and registered social landlords to provide new, varied forms of housing based on the needs of people currently in the private rented sector (that is, taking into account the housing factors important to them). This provision could include the formation of co-ops or co-housing, the provision of 'landlady-type' services and the purchase for rent of one-off houses in areas where people want to live.

- The government should commission a cost-
  benefit analysis of the value of these and other
  options compared with the cost of paying market-
  value rents through Housing Benefit. Reference
  rents control Housing Benefit expenditure by
  penalising the tenants: provision of attractive and
  varied alternative forms of housing in competition
  with the private rented sector would be a way of
  controlling rent levels that would benefit the
  tenants.
- The use of good housing option appraisal systems,
  together with the provision of information and
  advice, might help to prevent older people making
  inappropriate housing choices.

References

Action on Elder Abuse (2002) 'Questions and answers' (www.elderabuse.org.uk).

Age Concern London (2001) *Older people and Housing Benefit administration in London*, London: Age Concern London.

Anderson, A. (1999) 'Elder abuse: the clinical reality', in J. Pritchard (ed) *Elder abuse work: Best practice in Britain and Canada*, London: Jessica Kingsley.

ARLA (Association of Residential Letting Agents) (1997) 'Agreement', *Journal of the Association of Residential Letting Agents*, vol 4, no 2, July.

Ashton, G. (1994) *Action on Elder Abuse: Has it got its focus right?*, AEA Bulletin No 6, London: AEA

Audit Commission (2001) *Housing Benefit administration: Learning from inspection*, London: Audit Commission.

Audit Commission (2002) *Housing Benefit administration: The national perspective*, London: Audit Commission.

Bennett, G., Kingston, P. and Penhale, B. (1997) *The dimensions of elder abuse: Perspectives for practitioners*, London: Macmillan.

Better Government for Older People Steering Group Committee (2000) *All our futures*, Wolverhampton: Better Government for Older People Programme.

Biggs, S., Phillipson, C. and Kingston, P. (1995) *Elder abuse in perspective*, Buckingham: Open University Press.

Brammer, A. and Biggs, S. (1998) 'Defining elder abuse', *Journal of Social Welfare and Family Law*, vol 20, no 3, pp 285-304.

Brenton, M., Heywood, F. and Lloyd, L. (2002) *Housing and older people: Changing the viewpoint, changing the results*, London: London and Quadrant Housing Trust.

Coxon, J. (2002) 'Feel the benefit', *Inside Housing*, 12 April, p 29.

Crane, M. (1999) *Understanding older homeless people: Their circumstances, problems and needs*, Buckingham: Open University Press.

Crook, A.D.H. and Kemp, P. (1996) 'The revival of private rented housing in Britain', *Housing Studies*, vol 11, no 1, pp 51-68.

Crook, A.D.H. and Kemp, P. (1999) 'Financial institutions and private rented housing', Findings, York: Joseph Rowntree Foundation.

Crook, A.D.H., Hughes, J. and Kemp, P.A. (1995) *The supply of privately rented homes, today and tomorrow*, York: Joseph Rowntree Foundation.

DETR (Department for the Environment, Transport and the Regions) (1998) *1996 English House Condition Survey*, London: The Stationery Office.

DETR (2000a) *Housing Statistics 2000 Great Britain*, London: DETR.

DETR (2000b) *Quality and choice: A decent home for all*, Housing Green Paper, London: DETR.

DETR (2001a) *Quality and choice for older people's housing: A strategic framework*, London: DETR.

DETR (2001b) *Voluntary accreditation for private landlords*, Housing Research Summary No 144, London: The Stationery Office.

DoE (Department of the Environment) (1993) *English House Condition Survey 1991*, London: HMSO.

DoE (1995) *Our future homes: Opportunity, choice and responsibility*, Cm 2901, London: HMSO.

DoE (1996) *Private sector renewal: A strategic approach, Circular 17/96*, London: The Stationery Office.

DoH (Department of Health) (1998) *Modernising social services: Promoting independence, improving protection, raising standards*, London: The Stationery Office.

DoH (2000a) *No secrets: Guidance on developing and implementing multi-agency policies and procedures to protect vulnerable adults from abuse*, London: DoH.

DoH (2000b) *The NHS Plan*, London: The Stationery Office.

DoH (2001) *The National Service Framework for Older People*, London: DoH.

DTLR (Department of Transport, Local Government and the Regions) (2001a) *Housing in England 1999/00: A report of the 1999/2000 Survey of English Housing*, London: The Stationery Office.

DTLR (2001b) *Supporting People: Policy into practice*, London: DTLR/DoH/Home Office.

DTLR (2001c) *Selective licensing of private landlords: A Consultation Paper*, London: DTLR.

DTLR (2002) *Homelessness strategies: A good practice handbook*, London: DTLR.

Eastman, M. (1984) *Old age abuse* (2nd edn), Portsmouth: Age Concern.

Genn, H. (1999) *Paths to justice: What people do and think about going to law*, Oxford: Hart Publishing.

Gibson, M. and Langstaff, M. (1982) *An introduction to urban renewal*, London: Hutchinson.

Glendenning, F. (1993) 'What is elder abuse and neglect?', in P. Decalmer and F. Glendenning (eds) *The mistreatment of elderly people*, London: Sage Publications.

Hawes, D. (1997) *Older people and homelessness: A story of greed, violence, conflict and ruin*, Bristol: The Policy Press.

Heywood, F., Oldman, C. and Means, R. (2002) *Housing and home in later life*, Buckingham: Open University Press.

Inside Housing (2002) 'Incentives to shake up benefit', 18 October; 'Councils undecided over benefit reform pilot scheme', 1 November.

Jenkins, G., Asif, Z. and Bennett, G. (2000) *Listening is not enough: An analysis of calls to Elder Abuse Response – Action on Elder Abuse's national helpline*, London: Action on Elder Abuse.

Kemp, P., Wilcox, S. and Rhodes, D. (2002) *Housing Benefit reform: Next steps*, York: Joseph Rowntree Foundation.

Lau, E. and Kosberg, J. (1979) 'Abuse of the elderly by informal carer providers', *Ageing*, vol 299, pp 10-15.

Law Commission (1992) *Domestic violence and occupation of the family home*, Report No 207, London: HMSO.

Law Commission (1993) *Mentally incapacitated and other vulnerable adults: Public Law Protection*, Consultation Paper No 130, London: HMSO.

Law Commission (1995) *Mental incapacity*, Law Commission Report No 231, London: HMSO.

Law Commission (2002) *Renting homes, 1: Status and security*, Law Commission Consultation Paper No 162, London: The Stationery Office.

Leather, P. (1999) *Age File 99*, Kidlington: Anchor Trust.

Lord Chancellor's Department (1997) *Who decides? Making decisions on behalf of mentally incapacitated adults*, London: The Stationery Office.

Lord Chancellor's Department (1999) *Making decisions*, London: The Stationery Office.

McCreadie, C. (1996) *Elder abuse: Update on research*, London: Age Concern Institute of Gerontology.

Malpass, P. and Murie, A. (1999) *Housing policy and practice* (5th edn), Basingstoke: Macmillan.

Marsh, A., Niner, P., Cowan, D., Forrest, R. and Kennett, P. (2000) *Harassment and unlawful eviction of private rented sector tenants and park home residents*, London: DETR.

Mullins, D., Niner, P. and Riseborough, M. (1997) *Housing needs in Southend-on-Sea*, Birmingham, Centre for Urban and Regional Studies, University of Birmingham.

Offer, A. (1981) *Property and politics 1870-1914: Landownership, law, ideology and urban development in England*, Cambridge: Cambridge University Press.

ONS (Office for National Statistics) (1996) *Housing in England 1994/95*, London: The Stationery Office.

Pannell, J., Morbey, H. and Means, R. (2002) *Surviving at the margins: Older homeless people and the organisations that support them*, London: Help the Aged, HACT and Crisis.

Parry, S. and Means, R. (1999) *Getting through the maze: An evaluation of housing advice services for older people*, Bristol: The Policy Press.

Peakman, J. (1998) *Homelessness, transience and insecurity in the private rented sector: The effects of changes in Housing Benefit regulations*, London: Lewisham Organisation of Private Tenants.

Penhale, B. (1993) 'The abuse of elderly people', *British Journal of Social Work*, vol 23, no 2, pp 95-112.

Pillemer, K. (1996) 'Risk factors in elder abuse: results from a case-control study', in K. Pillemer and R. Wolf (eds) *Elder abuse: Conflict in the family*, Dover: Auburn House.

Pritchard, J. (2000) *The needs of older women: Services for victims of elder abuse and other abuse*, Bristol/York: The Policy Press/Joseph Rowntree Foundation.

Rugg, J. and Rhodes, D. (2001) *Chains or challenges? The prospects for better regulation of the private rented sector*, London and Coventry: British Property Federation and Chartered Institute of Housing.

Shelter (1999) *Licensing HMOs: An initial response*, London: Shelter.

Shelter (2002) *Private renting: A new settlement. The report of the Commission on the Private Rented Sector*, London: Shelter.

Slater, P. (2001) 'Preventing the abuse of vulnerable adults: social policy and research', *Journal of Social Policy*, vol 30, no 4, pp 673-84.

SSI (Social Services Inspectorate) (1993) *No longer afraid: The safeguard of older people in domestic settings*, London: HMSO.

Tarn, J. (1973) *Five per cent philanthropy: An account of housing in urban areas between 1840 and 1914*, Cambridge: Cambridge University Press.

Tinker, A., McCreadie, C. and Salvage, A. (1993) *The information needs of elderly people – An exploratory study*, London: Age Concern Institute of Gerontology.

Trickett, L. (1995) *Landlord and Agent Survey: Implications for the private rented sector*, Birmingham: Birmingham City Council.

Wilcox, S. (2000) *Housing Finance Review 2000/2001*, York: Joseph Rowntree Foundation.

Appendix:
Key informants

Statutory agencies

Tenants' rights officers, private tenancy team

Tenancy relations officers

Housing advice manager

Policy officer

Enforcement officers

Environmental health officers

Homeless action plan coordinator

Homeless services manager

Housing Benefits manager

Rent officers, Rent Service

Private and voluntary agencies

Outreach worker, an ethnic minority welfare association

Project coordinator, an ethnic minority welfare association

Roman Catholic priest working with an ethnic minority welfare association

Organiser of a community support and advice centre

Representative of a private landlords association

Members of local authority forum for private landlords

Solicitors of housing aid and legal centre

Older persons worker, specialist housing advice agency

Director of a local voluntary agency for homeless people

Estate agents and managing agents

The Elderly Accommodation Counsel

Director/advice and information manager of regional Age Concern offices

Local representative of Shelter